WITHDRAWN

HARVARD LIBRARY

WITHDRAWN

YOUNG REINHOLD NIEBUHR

His Early Writings, 1911–1931

Edited by William G. Chrystal
Foreword by John C. Bennett

YOUNG REINHOLD NIEBUHR

YOUNG REINHOLD NIEBUHR

His Early Writings, 1911–1931

*Edited and with an Introduction
by William G. Chrystal*

The Pilgrim Press
New York

BR
50
.N465
1982
cop. 2

Copyright © 1977 William G. Chrystal

All rights reserved. No part of this book may be reproduced in any manner without the written permission of the publisher, except in the case of brief quotations embodied in articles and reviews.

Thanks are due to the Fleming H. Revell Company of Old Tappan, New Jersey, for permission to reprint "Tyrant Servants," in Ralph Milton Pierce (editor), *Preachers and Preaching in Detroit*. New York: Fleming H. Revell Company, 1926, pp. 149-159, and also to the Oral History Research Office of Columbia University, under the direction of Louis M. Starr, for permission to quote from *The Reminiscences of Reinhold Niebuhr*. New York: Columbia University Oral History Research Office, 1972, on pp. 5-6 and p. 11.

Library of Congress Cataloging in Publication Data

Niebuhr, Reinhold, 1892-1971.
   Young Reinhold Niebuhr, his early writings, 1911-1931.

  Reprint. Originally published: Saint Louis, Mo.:
Eden Pub. House, c1977.
    Includes bibliographical references and index.
    1. Theology—Addresses, essays, lectures.
I. Chrystal, William G., 1947-   II. Title.
BR50.N465 1982   280'.4'0924   81-23421
ISBN 0-8298-0607-5 (pbk.)   AACR2

The Pilgrim Press, 132 West 31 Street, New York, NY 10001

To Mary, Shelley and Sarah

CONTENTS

Preface by Robert T. Fauth	9
Acknowledgments	11
Foreword by John C. Bennett	13
Introduction by William G. Chrystal	17
1. The Attitude of The Church Towards Present Moral Evils (1911)	41
2. Religion: Revival and Education (1913)	46
3. Yale—Eden (1914)	53
4. An Anniversary Sermon (1915)	59
5. That They May All Be One (1915)	64
6. A *Reformationsfest* Sermon (1915)	69
7. The Scylla and Charybdis of Teaching (1916)	74
8. The Future of Our Seminaries (1917)	79
9. A Modern Sunday School (1917)	84
10. The Present Day Task of the Sunday School (1918)	88
11. A Message from Reinhold Niebuhr (1918)	95
12. Where Shall We Go? (1919)	101
13. In Rebuttal, by the Author of "Where Shall We Go?" (1919)	109
14. Educational Principles in Church Schools (1919)	112
15. The Keryx and Our Educational Institutions (1920)	116
16. Shall a Minister Have an Education? (1921)	119
17. A Trip Through the Ruhr (1923)	124
18. Germany in Despair (1923)	128
19. The Despair of Europe (1923)	132
20. The Youth Movement of Germany (1923)	137

21. America and Europe (1923)	141
22. On Academic Vagabondage (1924)	145
23. The Dawn in Europe (1924)	151
24. Berlin Notes (1924)	154
25. Is Europe on the Way to Peace? (1924)	157
26. Our Educational Program (1924)	160
27. Tyrant Servants (1926)	165
28. Winning the World (1926)	174
29. An Aristocracy of Spiritual and Moral Life (1928)	179
30. Youth and Religion (1928)	190
31. Christianizing International Relations (1928)	199
32. The Traditions of the Fathers and the Virtues of the Children (1929)	209
33. Religion and Poetry (1930)	220
34. Christianity at the Dawn of a New Era (1931)	227
35. Christian Education and Society (1931)	235
Index	245

List of Illustrations

(Facing page 119)

Gustav Niebuhr
Edward J. Hosto
The Niebuhr family in Lincoln, Illinois
Reinhold Niebuhr as a co-manager of the Elmhurst Baseball Team
Reinhold and Richard Niebuhr at Eden
Reinhold Niebuhr as an Eden Seminary graduate, 1913
Bethel Evangelical Church as it appeared in 1915
Reinhold Niebuhr in 1918

PREFACE

In the records of Eden Theological Seminary, it is written that on June 11, 1913, a class of twenty-three students was *Ins Amt entlassen*—discharged into the office (of ministry). Among these was Reinhold Niebuhr.

During his Eden years, Niebuhr had contributed various articles to *The Keryx*, a student publication of the Seminary. In the time immediately following, as a graduate student at Yale, and as a pastor of Bethel Church, Detroit, Michigan, his brief, incisive articles continued to appear in *The Keryx*, later in the denominational journal, *The Evangelical Herald*, and in several other publications.

Much of this material is today available only in the Archives of the Evangelical Synod of North America—one of the constituent bodies forming the United Church of Christ—located at Eden. William Chrystal has assembled thirty-five of these early writings and published addresses and has edited them for this volume.

In it one can trace the early development of Niebuhr's thought and observe his wide-ranging interests, his marvelous blending of critical analysis and genuine appreciation for the Evangelical heritage whence he came and which marked the denomination in which he served, and the prophetic vision which in later years contributed so much to his greatness.

We, at Eden, appreciate the graciousness with which Ursula Niebuhr has given her blessing to this publication, and we offer it as an important addition to the Niebuhr writings in the hope that it will be helpful to scholars and meaningful to all those who remember Reinhold Niebuhr with admiration and affection.

ROBERT T. FAUTH, *President*
Eden Theological Seminary

ACKNOWLEDGMENTS

The essays in this collection resurfaced when I was attending Eden Theological Seminary and also working as Archivist in the Eden Archives. Most of these essays were found over the course of a summer by laboriously going through countless volumes of unindexed periodicals and publications. My systematic effort grew out of the discovery of some of Niebuhr's student writings in *The Keryx*, and soon led to a search through surprisingly diverse material. It quickly became apparent that this was a much larger body of writings than had been imagined, and of considerably greater importance. Thus, having been especially encouraged by Professor D. B. Robertson of Syracuse University to collect them into a single volume for the benefit of wider scholarship, I set about this task with the endorsement of the Eden Seminary faculty. To the Seminary faculty I am thankful for their affirmation of this work and confidence in me.

Mrs. Ursula Niebuhr not only provided permission for the use of the essays in this collection, but has been a patient correspondent, clarifying and enlarging my understanding of her husband's activities. Christopher Niebuhr, too, has been gracious in his assistance, and I remember with joy our shared visit to some of the scenes of his father's childhood. President Fauth, who kindly consented to write the Preface, not only brought to light several of the items presented here, but also affirmed this work at every turn. A long-time student of Niebuhr's thought and former pastor of Bethel Church in Detroit, he is also very much in the irenic tradition of another Eden President, Dr. Samuel D. Press.

Several members of the Eden faculty provided considerable assistance. Professor Lowell Zuck, Church Historian and Librarian of the Eden Archives, has helped in more ways than can be expressed, as has Professor Allen O. Miller, who introduced me to Niebuhr's thought and who first directed me "to see what might be down there in the Archives." Dean Walter Brueggemann read the work and provided assistance at critical points. Aside from his well-known Old Testament activities he is also a keen historian of Eden and its cherished traditions.

Dr. Carl E. Schneider, the dean of Evangelical Synod historians, spent long hours acquainting me with his seemingly-limitless knowledge, and he also provided warm reminiscences of his fellow student, Reinhold Niebuhr, as did Niebuhr's classmate Dr. Theophil H. Twente. To them both I am deeply indebted.

My special thanks also go to Dr. and Mrs. Elmer Hoefer and Mr. Raymond Gimbel of Lincoln, Illinois; Professor Richard Scheef of Eden Theological Seminary; Mrs. Ruth Rasche of St. Louis; Mrs. June Bingham and Professor Paul Lehmann. Catherine Keller's skillful translation of Niebuhr's two German sermons *gratis* amid a full pastoral schedule is yet another cause for rejoicing that she is my friend.

I likewise am indebted to Professor John C. Bennett for his willingness to read this material and prepare a Foreword. It is but another example of the graciousness for which he has become known.

The essays in this collection are presented in simple chronological order—with one exception that only serves to keep a series of European writings in sequence. Editorial work has been kept to a minimum as well. The purpose of this volume is to acquaint scholars with unknown facets of Niebuhr's career, and the Introduction is merely intended to render a better setting for understanding the essays themselves.

William G. Chrystal
1977

FOREWORD

By John C. Bennett

These early writings of Reinhold Niebuhr are an important source for understanding the religious and intellectual backgrounds of his later commitments and developed thought. They enable us to realize the depth of his roots in the Church by way of his own denomination, The Evangelical Synod, which has had its own unique history. He saw that this denomination should be ecumenical in spirit and in relationships and he early made suggestions for its union with the Reformed Church in the United States which finally took place. His ministry in Detroit was fully ecumenical in spirit but he remained very active in the affairs of the Evangelical Synod. This comes out in the attention he gives to the denominational problems of religious education. The period of these writings was a time of "Religious Education" as a pioneering movement of great strength. Those who knew him only when he was most sophisticated and most active in public life were always impressed by the depth and warmth of his piety. Readers of the *Leaves from the Notebook of a Tamed Cynic* have always known about the richness of his satisfactions in the pastoral ministry and how important this was to him and these writings supplement the *Leaves* in revealing the roots of his piety and of his involvement in the Church. I must confess that I find few traces of cynicism in this material that belongs to the same period as the *Leaves!* Knowledge about his denomination which is conveyed in the Editor's Introduction provides one clue to Niebuhr's later theology: Luther was an important influence in his denomination but it was not confessionally Lutheran. This explains his emphasis on Luther and the freedom with which he approached Luther.

YOUNG REINHOLD NIEBUHR: HIS EARLY WRITINGS, *1911-1931*

Those who knew Niebuhr later learned from him about the limitations of his early experience of higher education and of the formal handicaps they had created for his academic standing at Yale, but these writings reveal very vividly the degree of his dissatisfaction at the time with his college which he thought no better than a high school. His early seminary experience was redeemed by one great teacher. The distance between these academic handicaps and his later intellectual achievements is of great interest. The fact that he did not do advanced graduate work after he was fully accepted for it at Yale in spite of the handicaps makes one wonder what would have happened if he had gone the usual graduate school route. It is possible that his originality and perhaps more his intellectual adventures as a generalist that resulted in insights which a variety of specialists admired in their own field would have been less remarkable. He often said that he was not a scholar but he has kept many scholars busy writing about him. Though he did not work for a Ph.D. there are few recent thinkers about whom so many Ph.D. theses have been written. It is significant that many of these are cross-disciplinary studies.

I think that we gain from these early writings a better knowledge than we have had of the nature of his early liberalism. His expectations of *Christian* solutions of social problems were in line with those of the liberalism that he later disavowed and we learn more about them from the writings before 1929 than we have known. The changes which led up to his *Moral Man and Immoral Society* in 1932 begin to appear in the latest of these writings but they are less pronounced than I would have expected. His reflections on Europe after the First World War expand considerably what we have in the *Leaves*. Several of these writings give a more complete view of his support of that war than we get in the *Leaves* and this is important for the history of his relationship to pacifism. I think that what was at

FOREWORD

stake in the Second World War was so much more fateful than what was at stake in the First War that we cannot regard his strong support of the former as a replay of this earlier experience. Also, the intervening pacifist period made it more difficult for him to support any war.

These writings provide early intimations of Niebuhr's later stress which was so great on the limits of rational systems, on the role of the super-rational, on poetry and myth in religious understandings. Both in these writings and in the *Leaves* we see the early stages of his life-long struggle to express his faith in relation to both "mystery and meaning." Also in both we have proof of his early commitment to social justice and of the early presence of that searching honesty and what was later called realism especially in his self-criticism and in his criticism of the Church.

Students of Reinhold Niebuhr now and in the future will be grateful that these early writings have been made so readily available.

INTRODUCTION

By William G. Chrystal

Reinhold Niebuhr has been called the "greatest native-born Protestant theologian since Jonathan Edwards."[1] The author of 20 books and an encyclopedic body of shorter writings, he is certainly America's best known modern religious thinker. But in spite of already being the subject of several biographies, at least a dozen book-length theological studies and countless articles and dissertations, it is apparent that serious study of his life and work has really only begun.[2]

This volume, which might appear as another intrusion into the already-proliferated collections of Niebuhr's shorter writings, seeks to broaden the present understanding of Reinhold Niebuhr's development by focusing upon his early years. It

---

[1] Bob E. Patterson, *Reinhold Niebuhr*. Waco: Word Books, 1977, p. 13. Hans Morgenthau found him to be "the greatest living political philosopher of America, perhaps the only creative political philosopher since Calhoun." See Hans Morgenthau, "The Influence of Reinhold Niebuhr in American Political Life and Thought," in H.R. Landon (ed.), *Reinhold Niebuhr: A Prophetic Voice in Our Times*. Greenwich: Seabury, 1962, p. 109. In his "Intellectual Autobiography," Niebuhr's claim is characteristically modest: "I cannot and do not claim to be a theologian. I have taught Christian Social Ethics for a quarter of a century and have also dealt in the ancillary field of 'apologetics.' " See Reinhold Niebuhr, "Intellectual Autobiography," in C.W. Kegley and R.W. Bretall (eds.), *Reinhold Niebuhr: His Religious, Social and Political Thought*. New York: Macmillan, 1956, p. 3.

[2] Nonetheless, the following three major biographies provide an excellent introduction to Niebuhr: June Bingham, *Courage to Change*. New York: Scribner's, 1961; Ronald H. Stone, *Reinhold Niebuhr: Prophet to Politicians*. Nashville: Abingdon, 1972; and Paul Merkley, *Reinhold Niebuhr: A Political Account*. Montreal: McGill-Queens University Press, 1975.

takes the context in which he grew, that of the German Evangelical Synod of North America, as its starting point. It is composed of writings known only to a limited number of Synod pastors of an earlier generation that have largely been culled from its Archive. They are unknown to Niebuhr scholars and thereby enlarge considerably the corpus of his early works. Here, one is able to see Niebuhr develop from the age of eighteen onward, both by ascertaining his wide range of interests and by studying the actual documents which depict growth his later autobiographical accounts merely mention.[3] This collection, when combined with his other early writings, makes it possible to study Niebuhr's pre-Union Seminary maturation in greater detail, and likewise, serves to correct many inaccuracies contained in earlier research.[4]

Aside from the general treatises in this collection that provide a new picture of the embryonic theologue, the reader will quickly discern the denominational focus of many of these writings. Niebuhr's early development took place within a particular and rather unique context. Indeed, his deep commitment to his own religious communion is evident in these works, and it is possible to see that Niebuhr's labor within the German Evangelical Synod of North America actually provided his initial entree into inter-denominational circles.

Hopefully, this volume demonstrates that it is within Niebuhr's own denominational context that one must view his early growth, both as he implicity embraced some of its tenets

---

[3] Aside from autobiographical reflection in several articles, there are two principal sources: "Intellectual Autobiography," in Kegley and Bretall (eds.), *op. cit.*, pp. 3-23, and *The Reminiscences of Reinhold Niebuhr*. New York: Columbia University Oral History Research Office, 1972.

[4] The reader is encouraged to check details in this Introduction—which have been verified with official Evangelical Synod records—against other material found elsewhere.

INTRODUCTION

and as he rejected others. Before a balanced understanding of the early Reinhold Niebuhr can emerge, one must first gain some insight into the denomination in which he grew and was nurtured.

I

The German Evangelical Synod of North America *(Die Deutsche Evangelische Synode von Nord-Amerika)* was a product of the 16th Century Protestant Reformation and its subsequent liberalization as a result of the Enlightenment. But it also contained elements of a traditional piety that were often expressed in benevolent mission activity. At the same time, however, the Synod was an indigenous American phenomenon, occasioned by the extensive German immigration into the Mississippi Valley in the decades preceding the Civil War.

These settlers, who initially clustered in the area around St. Louis, were a mixed lot. Many were Rationalists, openly hostile to religious institutions. The greater number, however, were inheritors of a traditional piety with German Lutheran and Reformed roots that longed for organized church life. Their plight was soon recognized by a group of New Englanders who feared that without Protestant Churches the region might either lack earnest religion altogether, or worse yet, become a Catholic stronghold. As a result, a call was issued to the Basel Mission House to send pastors who could serve on the frontier. Likewise, various German and Swiss pastors who had been bound for other work in America were pressed into service by the immigrants themselves.[5]

---

[5] An extensive body of literature on the German Evangelical Synod of North America exists, but it is not known much beyond the confines of the

YOUNG REINHOLD NIEBUHR: HIS EARLY WRITINGS, *1911-1931*

Early in their independent existence the pastors of some of these congregations recognized a need for broader organization, and on October 15, 1840, six of them met in response to an invitation issued by Louis Nollau, pastor of a small congregation of German immigrants just outside of St. Louis in Gravois settlement (now Mehlville, Missouri). Although their intent was merely to organize for their own mutual support, they nonetheless drew up a brief confessional statement which by 1848 had been expanded into a form that remained the foundation of the Synod throughout its denominational existence:

> The German Evangelical Church Society of the West, as a part of the Evangelical Church, defines the term 'Evangelical Church' as denoting that branch of the Christian Church, which acknowledges the Holy Scriptures of the Old and New Testaments as the Word of God, the sole and infallible guide of faith and life, and accepts the interpretation of the Holy Scriptures as given in the symbolic books of the Lutheran and the Reformed Church, the most important being: The Augsburg Confession, Luther's and the Heidelberg Catechisms, in so far as they agree; but where they disagree the German Evangelical Church Society of the West adheres strictly to the passages of Holy

---

denomination itself. Thus, one important aspect of this study is to list them for the benefit of future scholarship. The most complete account of the beginnings of the Synod is Carl E. Schneider, *The German Church on the American Frontier*. St. Louis: Eden Publishing House, 1939. The chief disadvantage of this well-documented work is that it only covers the period up to 1866. However, the reader can follow the Synod through its somewhat complicated history by studying the relevant chapters in David Dunn et al, *A History of the Evangelical and Reformed Church*. Philadelphia: The Christian Education Press, 1961. Among the older histories the following are most useful: Albert Schory, *Geschichte der Deutschen Evangelischen Synode von Nord-Amerika*. St. Charles, Missouri, 1889; Albert Muecke, *Geschichte der Deutschen Evangelischen Synode von Nord-Amerika*. St. Louis: Eden Publishing House. 1915; and H. Kamphausen, *Geschichte des Religiösen Lebens in der Deutschen Evangelischen Synode von Nord-Amerika*. St. Louis: Eden Publishing House, 1924.

INTRODUCTION

Scriptures bearing on the subject and avails itself of the liberty of conscience prevailing in the Evangelical Church.[6]

Thus, the *Deutsche Evangelische Kirchenverein des Westens* which grew out of this meeting was not an attempt to formulate a new creed but, rather, to hold to a harmony which could be synthesized from the two major Reformation traditions. In this way, they embraced the prevalent Prussian model of union,[7] but placed it in a framework that had "a form of government which was distinctly American."[8]

The idea of bringing together the Reformed and Lutheran Churches had come about in Prussia in 1817 on the three hundredth anniversary of the Reformation. King Frederick William III, anxious for an increased sense of Prussian unity, reasoned that religious union was an important first step. Under Schleiermacher's influence a new understanding of the Reformation became possible and the traditionally divisive doctrinal differences, the King declared, no longer warranted separation into two communions. Indeed, in following years this union church spread into a number of other German regions.

The *Kirchenverein* did not long remain a pastoral association. In 1849 a St. Louis church applied for membership in the Society and was received. Soon, many other churches affiliated in like manner. Between 1858 and 1877 mergers with other similarily-established church bodies enabled rapid growth, and

---

[6] Quoted in F.H. Graeper, "The German Evangelical Synod of North America," in *The Evangelical Church*. St. Louis: Eden Publishing House, 1912, pp. 30-31.
[7] Schneider, *op. cit.*, p. 110, notes the following: "Any uncertainty as to the meaning of the term 'Evangelical' was removed by the simple subscription to the symbolic writings of 'our Evangelical mother church in Germany . . .'" This apparently took place at the first meeting.
[8] Graeper, *op. cit.*, p. 30.

by 1883 the resulting German Evangelical Synod of North America had grown to include 427 pastors and 535 churches. And as immigration continued the number steadily climbed. By 1915 there were 1,074 pastors and 1,381 churches.

Almost from its inception the *Kirchenverein* had taken an activist position with respect to education and benevolent missions. By 1850 the denominational Seminary (now Eden) and newspaper *(Der Friedensbote)* were founded.[9] In the following years a number of hospitals were built and a deaconess order was established to provide nursing care. In later years homes for orphans, elderly people, and the "feeble-minded" were likewise erected. To be sure, this kind of activity was a direct result of the *Missionshaus* education received by many of the early immigrant pastors who had viewed such *Innere-Mission* programs in their native lands.

Like many other immigrant churches, the German Evangelical Synod of North America faced special problems in America. While it had carefully met the needs of the foreign-born, growing numbers of second generation Americans became increasingly dissatisfied. "Americanization" became a rallying cry for many of them while their fathers and mothers grasped even more tightly to traditional ways. Indeed, this is best seen in the widespread controversy over maintaining the German language even though it was ceasing to be the language of the younger generation. Continuing German immigration in the later nineteenth century complicated the problem, which was only actually resolved by the First World War itself.

---

[9] The first Seminary or *Prediger-Seminar* was officially known as the "German Evangelical Missouri College." Nestled in the hills near Marthasville, Missouri, it trained seminarians until 1883 when a new Seminary was built in North St. Louis near a railroad station called "Eden Station"— hence the Seminary's name. "New Eden" in Webster Groves, Missouri (South St. Louis County), was built in 1924 and was the special vision of Dr. S.D. Press.

INTRODUCTION

Reinhold Niebuhr was born into the German Evangelical Synod of North America at a time when it was being torn by the whole process of Americanization, and he himself was to play a significant role in its resolution. Thus, his own development cannot be measured apart from the Evangelical Synod, not only because his struggles within it helped to mold his thought, but especially because its idea of the "union" of Luther and Calvin—of Lutheran *innerlichkeit* with the "moralism" of American Calvinism—became central in his own quest for truth.[10]

II

When he was in his 80's Dr. Samuel D. Press, Niebuhr's "Mark Hopkins" and close friend, learned to type.[11] Blindness had made it impossible for him to continue writing, but this way he could listen while his wife read to him and later sit at his typewriter and reflect upon what he had heard. One day he typed these words from Goethe:

Vom Vater hab ich die Statur,
des Lebens ernste Fuehrung;
Von Mutter hab ich die Froh-Natur
die Lust zum Fabulieren.

And in parentheses he noted, "This fits R.N. to a T."[12]

---

[10] This motif is so central to Niebuhr's thought it is often overlooked. But it is this very understanding which prompted the following remark in *Reflections on the End of an Era:* "In my opinion adequate spiritual guidance can come only through a more radical political orientation and more conservative religious convictions than are comprehended in the culture of our era." See *Reflections on the End of an Era.* New York: Scribner's, 1934, p. ix.

[11] Niebuhr refers to Press as his "Mark Hopkins" in both the "Intellectual Autobiography," *op. cit.*, p. 4, and in *The Reminiscences of Reinhold Niebuhr, op. cit.*, p. 11. In the latter account, however, Press is not specifically named.

[12] This was found among a number of typewritten autobiographical reflections done by Dr. Press in 1961.

In Goethe's aphorism Dr. Press found a key to Reinhold Niebuhr's development. Gustav Niebuhr, the father of Hulda, Reinhold and Richard, had come to America in reaction to his father's authoritarianism. After working as a farm hand he entered Eden Theological Seminary and completed his studies in 1885. He was ordained in St. Louis on May 31, 1885, and was assigned to Dixon, California, to assist the Synod's pioneer missionary, Edward J. Hosto, organizing congregations in the far west. On May 8, 1887, he married Lydia Hosto in Whitmore, California, and together they helped to found the first Evangelical Synod Church on the Pacific coast.[13]

Lydia Hosto Niebuhr was the daughter of Edward Hosto. Hosto had begun training in the Barmen *Missionshaus* at the age of 18, but had not been able to complete his training as a result of illness. After immigration to the U.S. because he learned pastors were needed, he taught school in Alhambra, Illinois, and preached in a small church on Sundays. By undertaking a course of study he was able to be ordained into the *Kirchenverein des Westens* in 1860. While serving in Maeystown, Illinois, Hosto was a founder of the "German Evangelical Immigrant Society for the Founding of Evangelical Congregations on the Pacific Coast," which encouraged Evangelical families to take advantage of the Homestead Act and move to California. In fact, Hosto was sent to California in 1884 as the Synod's first missionary, and in a five-year stay organized eight congregations.[14]

Lydia Niebuhr who has been called the "queen bee of Amer-

---

[13] Obituary in *Messenger of Peace*, Vol. XII, No. 10 (May 15, 1913), pp. 4-5.

[14] General biographical material comes from Hosto's obituary, *Messenger of Peace*, Vol. XI, No. 21 (November 1, 1912), p. 4. On his activities in forming the *deutsche evangelische Emigranten-Verein zur Gründung von evangelischen Gemeinden an der Pacifickküste* see *Der Friedensbote*, Vol. XXXV, No. 7 (1 April 1884), p. 53.

INTRODUCTION

ican theology," primarily because of her children's accomplishments, worked as an assistant to three generations of Hosto/Niebuhr ministers. As Reinhold Niebuhr later recalled, she had played a great role in his own ministry:

> She was a remarkable person who was kind of an assistant to my grandfather and then to my father, and subsequently to me, because in the early years of my ministry my father had died and my mother came to keep house for me. In my first parish in Detroit she was, in effect, a parish deaconess. She ran the women's meetings. She had great organizational skill.[15]

Lydia Niebuhr was born in Breese, Illinois, on December 25, 1869, and her entire life was spent deeply within the church. She became known in the Evangelical Synod as an expert on Sunday school work. Twice she spoke at the Synod's National Sunday School Conventions.[16] Most of all, however, Lydia Niebuhr was unostentatious and filled with joy and understanding. In 1953 Lindenwood College in St. Charles, Missouri, awarded her the degree of Doctor of Humanities.[17] It was the only award she ever received except for the knowledge that must come from a life enriched by service.

The union of Gustav Niebuhr and Lydia Hosto was, as Dr. Press noted, a blending of stature and joy, of leadership and vision. Both possessed a deep piety, yet valued raising their children in an atmosphere of freedom. In all respects, Gustav Niebuhr was a scholar and encouraged scholarship among his children.[18] But he was also decisive and took firm stands on

---

[15] *The Reminiscences of Reinhold Niebuhr*, op. cit., pp. 5-6.

[16] She spoke at the Second and Third National Conventions held on July 24-29, 1919 and June 28 to July 3, 1923 respectively.

[17] For a warm portrait of Mrs. Niebuhr see Ralph C. Abele, "A Woman Named Lydia . . ." *United Church Herald*, Vol. 2, No. 17 (September 17, 1959), pp. 10-12.

[18] See June Bingham, op. cit., p. 58. Reinhold Niebuhr learned Greek from his father.

25

social issues.[19] Gustav Niebuhr was a denominational leader. He was President of the Synod's North Illinois District, a founder of the Emmaus Homes at Marthasville and St. Charles, Missouri, and he helped establish the parish deaconess movement.[20] There is no doubt that his death at age 50 cut short a promising career that had a marked influence on Reinhold Niebuhr.

III

Reinhold Niebuhr moved to Lincoln, Illinois in 1902. Gustav Niebuhr had been unanimously called to the pastorate of St. John's Evangelical Church and simultaneously, to the superintendency of the newly-founded Deaconess Hospital. Since returning from California he had served two Evangelical Synod churches, Friedens in Wright City, Missouri—where Reinhold Niebuhr was born—and St. John's in St. Charles, Missouri.[21] As Reinhold explained, early on he wanted to follow in his father's footsteps: "You are the most interesting man in town," Gustav was told.[22]

The town of Lincoln, Illinois, is steeped in the memory of its namesake. "Certainly the town of Lincoln was named after

---

[19] Gustav Niebuhr wrote a pamphlet on the "Lodge Question" (*Logenfrage*) which was one of the most important social issues in German-American communities. See *Die Evangelische Synode von Nord-Amerika und die Logenfrage*. Herausgegeben auf Beschluss der Bloomington-Pastoralkonferenz, n.d.
[20] See the Memorial-Ausgabe of *Der Evangelische Diakonissen-Herold*, Vol. 7, No. 4 (Mai, 1913).
[21] Gustav Niebuhr served in Wright City from 1892-1895 and in St. Charles from 1895-1899. Following a brief trip to Germany he became the travelling representative of the Emmaus Homes at Marthasville and St. Charles. He served in this capacity from July of 1899 until he assumed the position in Lincoln, Illinois. He served two Utah Churches for several months in 1902 when they were without a pastor. This was at the request of the *Behörde für Innere Mission*.
[22] June Bingham, *op. cit.*, p. 58. Mrs. Bingham's account is laced with some delightful stories of Niebuhr's childhood.

INTRODUCTION

me," Abraham Lincoln remarked in 1858, "for I was named first."[23] As a young boy in Lincoln, Reinhold Niebuhr came under Abraham Lincoln's spell. The old Court House where Abe addressed a Republican gathering was replaced by a newer one, no doubt as the newly-arrived Niebuhr children watched. The old wooden Postville Court House where Lincoln had tried cases as a circuit lawyer, stood less than a mile from the Niebuhr home.[24] The town also remembered sadly, but with a touch of pride, that Lincoln's funeral train stopped at the old depot so that his friends might say good-by.

A combination of "genteel poverty," as Reinhold later called it, and a desire to prepare for the ministry in his denomination, necessitated attending the Synod's *Proseminar* at Elmhurst, Illinois, which provided considerable assistance to ministers' sons. Before leaving, however, he spent one year attending Lincoln High School. One of his Elmhurst and Eden classmates later believed that this additional year gave him a decided edge over his peers, many of whom merely had a grammar school background.[25]

At Elmhurst, Niebuhr was active in the band and as a manager of the baseball team. Academically, however, he apparently did not excel. He was not one of the three students in the Class of 1910 recognized for special achievement.[26]

---

[23] Quoted in *The Namesake Town: A Centennial History of Lincoln, Illinois*. Lincoln, Illinois: Feldman's Print Shop, August 27, 1953, p. 2. There can be no doubt that Niebuhr's deep regard for Lincoln grew in Lincoln, Illinois.

[24] Ironically, Henry Ford purchased the old Court House. In fact, he visited Lincoln in 1929 to inspect his purchase before removing it to Dearborn Village.

[25] This remark is contained in a tape-recorded reminiscence of Reinhold Niebuhr by Dr. Theophil H. Twente.

[26] See the *Jahrbuch des Evang. Proseminars, Studienjahr 1909-1910*, p. 28, for a list of the awards and the recipients. Niebuhr, who was christened Karl Paul Reinhold Niebuhr, sent a graduation announcement to Adam Denger, his former employer and owner of a store in Lincoln. The enclosed card reads, "Reinhold P. Niebuhr."

27

Niebuhr was later perturbed at the insufficiency of his Elmhurst training. As the equivalent of a German *gymnasium*, there was abundant work in the classics but little preparation in the sciences, history and English literature.[27] At that point in time Elmhurst was not an accredited school. No degrees were awarded, but instead a diploma was issued that had meaning only within the Evangelical Synod. This was a considerable source of embarrassment to Niebuhr at Yale. As he wrote Dr. Press in 1914,

> The more I see how highly scholarship is prized in other denominations the more the penny-wise attitude of our church makes me sore. But what we need more than several special students is a *college* education for all of our students. The more I look at the thing the more I see that I have been cheated out of a college education. Elmhurst is little more than a high school. I thought once that I lacked only the B.A. but I have found since that I lack the things that make up a B.A., philosophy, ethics, science and a real course in English . . . I don't know if I'll ever have a voice in our church but if I will have it will never be silent until our ministry receives an adequate education.[28]

A number of the writings in this collection are the fulfillment of that promise, beginning with "Yale—Eden," and culminating with "Shall a Minister Have an Education?". Indeed, in later years both Reinhold and H. Richard Niebuhr, who became President of Elmhurst College in 1924 in the first year an A.B. degree was offered, were among those who worked tirelessly to bring the Synod's educational institutions into line with other American colleges and universities.

---

[27] See *The Reminiscences of Reinhold Niebuhr, op. cit.*, p. 10.
[28] Reinhold Niebuhr letter to S.D. Press, March 3, 1914. Press' previous letter no doubt informed Niebuhr that two other Eden students would be joining him at Yale in the fall, Cornelius Krusé and Niebuhr's boyhood friend from Alhambra, Illinois, Henry Dinkmeyer. These were the "special students" to whom Niebuhr refers.

INTRODUCTION

When Reinhold Niebuhr entered Eden College (as it was then known) in the Fall of 1910, he was probably expecting a continuation of the boredom he had experienced at Elmhurst. Surprisingly, however, he found salvation in Dr. Samuel D. Press: "As is often the case, one teacher will redeem an institution for a youngster who otherwise wouldn't be interested," Niebuhr explained.[29] Dr. Press was a thorough-going scholar with an incredibly irenic spirit. After his death Niebuhr paid him the following tribute:

> President Samuel Press' life spanned a century but it is more important that the life of this charismatic personality was devoted to the Seminary for half a century. During that half-century generations of students were influenced by both his Christian faith, expressed in simple terms, and his theological learning which was encyclopedic. It spanned both Old and New Testament and systematic theology. I know that he first made both the prophet Amos and the apostle Paul a real influence in my religious life. Next to my father his influence on my life was so all pervasive that it is difficult to do justice to it. One can only thank God for his rich and creative life.[30]

Dr. Press had awakened Niebuhr's scholarly side. Press, who was the son of an Evangelical Synod pastor, was born near Cambria, Wisconsin on May 24, 1875. He attended Elmhurst and Eden and had served as a pastor in several Texas churches. In 1902-03 he studied in Berlin under Adolf von Harnack and Reinhold Seeberg as a result of having won a "Domstift scholarship" while at Eden. In 1908 he was called to Eden College as the first English Professor, teaching all of his courses in the language of the United States. He was also the

---

[29] *The Reminiscences of Reinhold Niebuhr, op. cit.,* p. 11.
[30] Reinhold Niebuhr letter to Robert Fauth, President of Eden Theological Seminary, August 21, 1967.

first native-born professor to serve at Eden.[31] One of his colleagues felt Press had been called to this position because of his "strong German background."[32] Yet Press was thoroughly American in his outlook, and while Niebuhr was a student, he took his "American Theology" course which concentrated on the contributions of Calvinism in America—which was, of itself, most unusual in a German-oriented school. When the Seminary's "Director," William Becker, died in 1919, Press was called to be the "President"—this change in title is itself illustrative of Press' thrust toward Americanizing Eden. He was President until 1941 and he continued teaching on a part-time basis until 1951.[33]

Reinhold Niebuhr was Eden's *Abschiedsredner* (Valedictorian) at graduation. His academic record was sound, and he had been one of two members of a debate team which defeated the team from the Missouri Synod's Concordia Seminary. He was a charter member of the group which began the student journal, *The Keryx*, and in his final year at Eden was its editor. The first article in this anthology, "The Attitude of The Church Towards Present Moral Evils," appeared in the first issue. Niebuhr was also active in student government and in a number of extracurricular activities. He was an officer in the Lincoln Lyceum, an English-language literary society, and was the winner of its first Thesis Contest, the text of which appeared in *The Keryx* and is included here. Reinhold Niebuhr's ability was apparent to the faculty and

---

[31] For a better description of Press' role at Eden see Carl E. Schneider, *History of the Theological Seminary of the Evangelical Church*, n.d., and Walter Brueggemann, *Ethos & Ecumenism, An Evangelical Blend: A History of Eden Theological Seminary, 1925-1975*. St. Louis: Eden Publishing House, 1975, pp. 1-7.

[32] Wilhelm L. Baur, *The Wanderer*. Elmhurst, Illinois, 1951, p. 84.

[33] Reinhold Niebuhr was a member of Eden's Board of Directors for nearly this same period of time. He served from 1923-1955.

INTRODUCTION

to his classmates, one of whom selected a sentence from the *Märchen von den sieben Schwaben* to appear with his picture in the graduation issue of *The Keryx:*

Hannemann! Geh du voran,
Du hast die grössten stiefel an.[34]

Gustav Niebuhr died on April 21, 1913, and Reinhold, who with Helmut Richard was present at the time, remained to supply his father's pulpit. He wrote his Eden classmates suggesting that they encourage the faculty to select another valedictorian because he had missed well over a month of classes while serving in Lincoln. His peers, however, insisted that the faculty's decision should stand.[35] Thus, on June 11, 1913, at the Class of 1913's *Schlussfeier*, Niebuhr delivered the valedictory address and received his diploma from Director Becker.

On June 29, 1913, he was ordained into the ministry of the German Evangelical Synod of North America by Wm. Theo. Jungk, a friend of Gustav Niebuhr's and Editor of the main denominational newspaper, *Der Friedensbote*. Assisting were two other friends, Theo. Kettlehut and George Goebel. Dr. Press also participated.[36] Thus, as an ordained minister, he continued to serve St. John's throughout the summer until leaving for New Haven.[37]

---

[34] *The Keryx*, Vol. III, No. 3 (June, 1913), p. 4.

[35] Minutes of May 13, 1913, *The Minutes of the Elmhurst Class of 1910/ Eden Class of 1913*. The student vote was unanimous.

[36] *Record of Ordinations for the German Evangelical Synod of North America*, p. 29. The date "1915" often appears for Niebuhr's ordination in various accounts.

[37] Among other things, Niebuhr confirmed a class that his father had taught. See *St. John Church, 1860-1960*. Lincoln, Illinois, p. 36.

IV

Even though they were written some forty years after he arrived in New Haven, Connecticut, Reinhold Niebuhr's "Intellectual Autobiography," and *Reminiscences* still contain hints of the excitement the young Niebuhr must have experienced in that intellectually-charged environment. Indeed, the very fact that he reminisced at such length about Yale would seem to bear this out. For the first time in his life, Niebuhr threw himself into his studies.

Niebuhr's decision to study at Yale was, as he later explained, heartily supported by his father who assumed it would be like a German University, and by Dr. Press. Press had found his own graduate study in Germany rewarding, and he therefore encouraged some of his students to go on for further study, beginning with Reinhold Niebuhr.

"Yale—Eden," written in the middle of Niebuhr's two years in the east, further elaborates on his impressions of Yale given later. Yet here, the freshness of his experience is readily apparent. For him, Yale was nearly ideal: "I must say that in my opinion it combines scholarship and real spirituality about as ideally as this can be done."[38]

At Yale, Niebuhr was most conscious of being a midwesterner, of recent immigrant stock, degreeless and a member of an unknown denomination. His professors, however, appeared to take no notice of all that made Niebuhr feel so insecure. Their genuine interest in him amazed Niebuhr, and even his German background proved advantageous as he reviewed untranslated works for his classmates. In 1914, he was awarded a B.D., his first academic degree. In 1915, he received his

---

[38] "Yale—Eden," *The Keryx*, Vol. IV, No. 5 (December, 1914), p. 2.

INTRODUCTION

highest earned degree, a Master of Arts, but instead of going on for a doctorate as Professor D.C. Macintosh encouraged, Niebuhr decided to enter the parish.

As he later indicated, his decision not to continue in school was reached for several reasons. Not only was he bored with epistemology, but he was also feeling increased pressure from his denomination. The largely-free Elmhurst and Eden education obligated him to serve an Evangelical Synod parish. In addition, his mother and sister were nearly destitute in Lincoln—Gustav Niebuhr's insurance having been exhausted—and they looked to Reinhold for support. Thus, on August 8, 1915, Niebuhr moved with his mother and sister Hulda to Detroit to assume the pastorate of Bethel Evangelical Church.

Bethel Church had been formed in September, 1912, by a June graduate of Eden Seminary, Paul R. Zwilling, who had been a co-manager of the Elmhurst baseball team with Reinhold Niebuhr. In March of 1914 a chapel was dedicated on Linwood and Lothrop Avenues for the congregation of 32 people, and, by the time Paul Zwilling left in July, 1915 to accept a call in Buffalo, New York, the membership had doubled.[39]

Soon after Niebuhr's arrival the German Evangelical Synod of North America celebrated its Diamond Jubilee. Twice that day Niebuhr preached, once in German and once in English, from prepared manuscripts. Both of these sermons are included in this collection and indicate the extent to which he was already concerned with issues of broad Christian understanding. Indeed, two weeks later, on Reformation Sunday, Niebuhr preached a *Reformationsfest* sermon in German, and it, too, appears here.

---

[39] *Anniversary Record Commemorating the Twenty-Fifth Anniversary of Bethel Evangelical Church.* Detroit, 1937, pp. 13-14.

YOUNG REINHOLD NIEBUHR: HIS EARLY WRITINGS, *1911-1931*

Certain aspects of Niebuhr's Detroit years have been described in great detail. Not only do his later reminiscences talk about this period at length, but in addition, one can consult his diary from that period, *Leaves from the Notebook of a Tamed Cynic*.[40] Nonetheless, there are several aspects of his work that have remained unknown to scholars. Of particular interest are Niebuhr's writings on Christian Education themes. He became an Associate Editor of a new denominational publication, *The Evangelical Teacher*, and contributed a number of pieces which were mainly devoted to the practical difficulties of Church School operation. In addition, Niebuhr was called upon occasionally to lecture before denominational conferences on Christian Education topics. A number of the items in this collection were made from stenographic transcripts taken at those conferences.

America's involvement in the First World War, however, provided Niebuhr his first major denominational role. In October, 1917, he was appointed Executive Secretary of the Evangelical Synod's War Welfare Commission, whose task was to maintain contact with Evangelical men in the service by providing denominational periodicals and literature, assigning Synod pastors to work in nearby army camps, and eventually, recruiting chaplains for the armed forces.[41]

His work with the War Welfare Commission forced Niebuhr to articulate his sense of national loyalty. The German Evangelical Synod of North America still was predominately a

---

[40] Reinhold Niebuhr, *Leaves from the Notebook of a Tamed Cynic*. Chicago: Willett, Clark & Colby, 1929.

[41] For a more complete discussion of Niebuhr's activities during this period see my article, "Reinhold Niebuhr and the First World War," *The Journal of Presbyterian History*, Vol. 55, No. 3 (Fall, 1977).

INTRODUCTION

German-speaking body, and a number of its pastors were sympathetic to Germany. This made the Synod's relations with the Government precarious at best. The two articles in this collection written during the war, "The Present Day Task of the Sunday School," and "A Message from Reinhold Niebuhr," were designed not only to provide a basic understanding of why American participation was essential, but also as a way to encourage further support within the churches. And, while these are important vehicles for understanding Niebuhr's own view of the First World War, it is also clear that they help fill in a critical period in his development. He was later to say that the war was responsible for creating his whole world view.[42] But in spite of a pacifist interlude following the First World War, it is apparent that the war had a profound and lasting effect. Indeed, "A Message from Reinhold Niebuhr," especially shows the extent to which his Second World War position was informed by this earlier experience.

As a result of his wartime service Niebuhr was introduced into inter-denominational circles. He owed his appointment with the War Welfare Commission to Dr. John Baltzer, President of the Synod. And in connection with this work, which also included attending the meetings of the General War Time Commission, Niebuhr was appointed as one of the Synod's delegates to the Federal Council of Churches. Likewise, the numerous lectures and speeches he had delivered across the country as a result of the war work had brought considerable notoriety, and from then on, Niebuhr was a sought-after speaker.

---

[42] See Reinhold Niebuhr, "What the War Did to My Mind," *Christian Century*, Vol. XLV, No. 39 (September 27, 1928), pp. 1161-1163.

V

Not only was the First World War a period in which American churches optimistically backed the war, but it was also a time in which church union loomed as a real possibility in a number of denominations. As his 1915 Anniversary Sermon on church unity demonstrated, Reinhold Niebuhr was keenly aware of the posibilities inherent in church union. No doubt because of this he was appointed by Dr. Baltzer as a delegate to the Conference on Organic Union of the Church which was called by the General Assembly of the Presbyterian Church in the U.S.A. in December, 1918.

This meeting literally filled Niebuhr with excitement, and he returned from Philadelphia and wrote "Where Shall We Go?", articulating his belief that the Evangelical Synod, when presented with the possibility of merger within the two main European Reformation traditions, must join with Calvinism. This proposal met with sharp rejection initially, but in the decade which followed, the debate continued. And as the merger of the Evangelical and Reformed Church was later to demonstrate, Niebuhr had prophetically predicted the pattern for union that eventually led to the formation of the United Church of Christ.

In the post-war period Niebuhr also renewed his call to improve the denominational educational institutions. Both *"The Keryx* and Our Educational Institutions," and "Shall a Minister Have an Education?", repeated his earlier arguments. Indeed, this latter article was directed against two professors of considerable stature and brought Niebuhr under harsh criticism once again. Still, his point had been made and it would only be a few years until Elmhurst bore all the signs of being an accredited college. "On Academic Vagabondage" also was developed as a vehicle to encourage better education among

INTRODUCTION

ministers in the denomination. Niebuhr probably believed that the provincialism he viewed in the Synod could best be dispelled by studying at other schools. His method of making that point in this piece was most unusual for him, however, though it undoubtedly had an effect, particularly on the Eden students.

In 1923 and 1924, Reinhold Niebuhr was selected to be a participant in the American Seminars led by Sherwood Eddy. Not only was this his first opportunity to delve deeply into the chaotic post-war European scene, but it also served to introduce him to several people who became close friends. Episcopal Bishop Will Scarlett, Kirby Page and Sherwood Eddy were all impressed with the young pastor who spoke German so fluently, and who also had impressive European connections through his denomination. Otto Dibelius proved most helpful to the group in Berlin. This was the result of Dr. Baltzer's close relationship with the Berlin church leader.[43]

The articles in this anthology, written as a result of Niebuhr's European trips, indicate a perceptive grasp of European politics. They clearly acknowledge his growing fear that civilization itself will be bankrupt if the European states fail to achieve a degree of harmony. As *Leaves from the Notebook of a Tamed Cynic* also later revealed, the 1923 trip to Germany was responsible for thrusting Niebuhr into the pacifist camp. The disparity between the situation in Germany, particularly

---

[43] Dr. Baltzer wrote Dibelius on June 12, 1923, telling him of Niebuhr's visit. In a letter to Dr. Baltzer on September 3, 1923, Niebuhr said, "Dr. Dibelius was very good to me and helped me very much to get in touch with the church leaders." On this trip Niebuhr hired a stenographer for Baltzer: "I almost sold my soul in getting permission at the consulate for her to come to America for I had to promise to be responsible for her in America without being able to tell that we had employed her as that is against the law. As it is also against the law for an unmarried man to be responsible for an unmarried girl I finally told the consul that it was really you and not I who was responsible and he let it slip through."

in the Ruhr, and the verbalized aims for which the war had been waged had been more than he could bear.

From the mid-twenties on, Rienhold Niebuhr became increasingly involved with international events and with questions of justice in American society.[44] He had moved out of denominational circles somewhat, and was now writing regularly on a national level. In 1925, he was offered an Associate Editor position with *Christian Century* which would have necessitated leaving Bethel Church. But when he wrote Dr. Baltzer announcing his intention to accept, the Synod President raised a question that caused Niebuhr to reconsider:

> I cannot say that I am altogether surprised at the offer, I can understand it and am thankful to you that you were so kind to let me in on this very personal affair of yours. I honor your confidence. Personally I would not like to step in your way, for I see possibilities for you for the future of our Church. But let me ask you, Brother Reinhold, do you wish to exchange your pulpit where the Lord certainly has blessed you and gave you the opportunity to influence a great many people connected and not connected with your church for an editorship?[45]

Thus, Niebuhr remained at Bethel Church for three more years. The many demands on his time were somewhat lessened, however, by the presence of an Assistant Pastor. Theodore C. Braun, Harold A. Pflug and Ralph Abele all served as assistants to Niebuhr.[46]

---

[44] The little-known article, "Tyrant Servants," is a classic example of the way in which his thought had developed at this point.

[45] Dr. John Baltzer letter to Reinhold Niebuhr, April 27, 1925. Niebuhr decided it would be possible to continue serving Bethel Church *and* write weekly for the *Christian Century.*

[46] Braun, who later was Editor of the *United Church Herald*, served from 1923-1925. Pflug, who became a Professor at Eden Seminary, was at Bethel from 1925-1927, and Abele, from 1927-1928. For many years he was the Pastor at St. Louis' Holy Ghost Church.

INTRODUCTION

In spite of his numerous interests and growing commitments, Niebuhr continued working within the denomination, although his editorial contributions decreased considerably. He was particularly sought after as a speaker at various synodical conventions. Indeed, most of the later pieces in this collection were delivered as addresses at meetings, some even after his move to Union Seminary. "Religion and Poetry," on the other hand, was prepared specifically for the synodical *Theological Magazine* in 1930. In many respects it is the most exciting article in the collection, for in it one is able to grasp Niebuhr's own understanding of the relationship of religious experience to rational understanding. It is, perhaps, the autobiographical piece that underlies so much of Niebuhr's work and tells one so much about him.

Even as a Professor at Union Seminary in New York City Niebuhr continued to exercise influence in the Evangelical Synod. Frequently he was called upon to write articles, deliver lectures and provide counsel, and whenever possible, he complied. Niebuhr owed a great deal to the denomination in which he had grown, and it, too, was indebted to him. His work in improving the Synod's educational institutions laid him bare to great criticism, but aided in the establishment of Elmhurst as an excellent college.[47] So, too, had he risked his reputation in suggesting the pattern for church union within the Synod, but it also developed along the lines he laid out.

---

[47] Needless to say, Niebuhr's long association with Eden Seminary was also influential. In 1950, when the faculty prepared a collection of essays in honor of Eden's Centennial, only two non-faculty members were asked to contribute. One, H. Richard Niebuhr, had once served on the Eden faculty and had even been Dean. The other was Reinhold Niebuhr. Soliciting his contribution was no doubt Eden's own way of thanking Reinhold Niebuhr for his many years of service. See Elmer J.F. Arndt (ed.), *The Heritage of the Reformation: Essays Commemorating the Centennial of Eden Theological Seminary*. New York: Richard R. Smith, 1950.

Niebuhr's debt was equally profound. The Evangelical Synod's unique synthesis of Luther and Calvin provided him with a remarkable environment in which to develop his own theology. And in this he was inestimably aided by the thorough-going scholarship of Dr. Samuel Press. Niebuhr also owed a great deal to the climate in which he grew. The yearning for Americanization which was expressed in the Synod in a number of ways, became a central drive in Niebuhr and had many consequences for his later development. Growing up as a German-American in the German Evangelical Synod of North America was both a provincial experience and a visionary one. And Niebuhr's early years were spent in rejecting the provincialism while at the same time embracing the visionary. In this he was not alone—indeed, the other leaders of the denomination were likewise similarly engaged—but in Niebuhr's case the result was to have a profound effect on all of American theology.

[The earliest of Niebuhr's writings appeared in the premiere issue of the Eden Theological Seminary student journal, *The Keryx*, in February, 1911. Its eighteen-year-old author was a charter staff member and, in his final year of Seminary (1912-13), served as Editor.]

I. The Attitude of The Church Towards Present Moral Evils

The Christian Church is an institution of divine origin and divine character, an agency through which man may hold communion with his Creator and a source from which he may draw nourishment for his spiritual life. However, it cannot, although it be divine, remain aloof from all secular and temporal problems which trouble mankind. It finds itself constantly in a surging sea of moral strife, and in a controversy between the morally right and the morally wrong it must necessarily take issue with the right. By the very nature of its doctrines and its principles the Church stands upon the right side of all moral questions taken collectively, but how far the Church should enter directly and specifically into any movement, which has as its aim the elimination of any moral or social evil, is a question every Christian should attempt to solve. Any activity in this direction puts the Church in the danger of becoming the advocator of moral principles rather than the teacher of the Gospel.

This danger the Church of to-day, especially the American Church, has not entirely avoided. We could not prove that it is the tendency of the modern Church to preach morality rather than religion, but there is without doubt at least a tendency within the Church in that direction. And the Church has been tempted in a most subtle manner by the conditions of our times. This is an age of moral awakening, for the danger of the low moral conditions of our people to the future of the state and nation is plainly evident to every thinker and a remedy for the evil is widely sought. The age is, moreover, also one of little philosophy and much superficiality, an age which sees not the cause and reasons of all things, but which widely scrambles for results. And such an age, too shallow to find in religion and Christianity the real root of morality and too superficial to recognize the spreading of the gospel of Jesus Christ as the real and primary duty of the Church, beckons it to abandon this most important work at least partly and to fight side by side with worldly forces and with their methods for a higher morality and better social conditions. It is a good cause! Why shouldn't the Church enlist in the fight?

To answer this question we must first clearly determine the exact relation of morality to religion. Morality in its broadest meaning, not as contrasted to libertinism and licentiousness, but morality, that system of duties and obligations which devolves upon every man as a unit force in society is born of religion and is related to it as effect is to cause. We may find morality outside of the Church's influence. We, of course, expect more of a Christian than mere civil virtue, morality, but that is at least one thing we rightfully expect. His morality is, moreover, not forced upon him, but spontaneous, and therefore lasting, and his example does not drive, but leads other men outside of the Church to higher moral standards, so that the influence of the Church is not confined to its members alone, but reaches all men and its religion is the root of all morality. To make more men Christians and all Christians truer would then be the only correct method by which we could achieve the aim of our day and start the fastly declining and degenerating morals on the

THE ATTITUDE OF THE CHURCH TOWARDS PRESENT MORAL EVILS

ascent. Unfortunately other methods are being used at the expense of this one in fighting present evils.

Some prominent present day evils and the tactics with which the Church is fighting for their elimination might be worth mentioning. The degeneracy of morals, and now we use that word in the narrower sense, and the consequent degeneracy of the family to which the ever increasing number of divorces testify; dishonesty in business, the ever widening breach between rich and poor and above all the curse of the saloon, these are some of the evils the elimination of which has become a serious problem. And we find many ministers of the gospel treating them as an economist or a practical statesman would treat them. They would curb immorality by more drastic laws and they ask the state to restrict divorces by forceful measures; they talk of the advisibility of honesty in business and demand of the state a closer surveillance over large corporations; they use the Church to champion their almost socialistic ideas about a greater equality between rich and poor brought about by state interference, and they become loud in their denouncement of the liquor traffic and in their demand to have this evil curbed. They are in short dealing with moral evils not as obstacles in the way of eternal life, but as a detriment to the state and nation. The measures which they urge would no doubt bring about a betterment in existing conditions, but it could not be permanent for they would but force a morality, a false virtue, on people who are at heart no better than before. Again we come to the truth that real morality can not come from without, but must come from within, from entirely changed hearts and ideals, and only one thing can change man's sinful heart, the gospel of Jesus Christ.

The immoral would be cleansed by Christ's love for them and for His sake they would change their life; the intemperate would receive strength from above in order that they might subdue their inordinate desires; the dishonest and unscrupulous would be captured by Christ's sincerity and truthfulness; those whom God had blessed with an abundance of worldly goods would become charitable towards their less fortunate brothers as they were overwhelmed more and more by Christ's charity for them, and rich and poor would be brothers as they felt their kinship as children of God. That would be a morality of a lasting kind and although such conditions may seem to be impossibly utopian they are really only a goal which should and can be attained if the Church will but use all the energy and influence at its command undiminished by any activity which is foreign to its nature and rightfully belongs in the domain of worldly institutions. It can be of the greatest service to society and to the state wihout being a detriment to itself.

Such misplaced activity on the part of the Church, however, is not only wrong because it is the wrong way to reach the desired end, a higher morality, but because that very end should and can not be the main one for the church. Better conditions on earth are but incidental and subservient to its paramount aim, the salvation of man. Morality, although it is an essential of a Christian's life, will alone neither lead to religion nor will it directly make man worthy of salvation. If we think of the phase of the modern tendency, to preach morality rather than religion, to make of the Church nothing but a society for the elimination of moral and social evils, the error of it takes on such monstrous proportions that we can no longer call it an error innocently committed but are forced to the conclusion that it is often but a sign of the death of spirituality within the Church. In order to conceal this death, morality, the outward manifestation of spirituality is used as a subterfuge. Truly there is but little difference between the

THE ATTITUDE OF THE CHURCH TOWARDS PRESENT MORAL EVILS

Pharisees of old and our present day moralist. Having lost the real essence of their religion, both cling to its fruits which, taken from the root, can have no life. The latter may uphold real civil virtues while the former had many false and inverted ones, but essentially both make the same mistake and the words of our Lord to the former are applicable to both: "But seek ye first the kingdom of God and his righteousness; and all these things shall be added unto you."

[The following essay was the "First Honor Thesis" in the Lincoln Lyceum Thesis Contest. The Lincoln Lyceum had been founded by Eden's first English-language Professor, Dr. Samuel D. Press, in 1909 as a literary society devoted to debate, writing and literary criticism in the vernacular. Prior to its establishment the only similar organization was the *Deutsche Literarische Verein*. Niebuhr was the first to win the Thesis Contest, written on a topic chosen by Dr. Press, and his entry was published in the June, 1913 issue of *The Keryx*.]

2. Religion: Revival and Education

All religion is life, and as a life its most predominant characteristic, its most important necessity, is development and perpetuation. Without perpetuation all life must ultimately die. Without growth life is already death. A living thing will grow unconsciously if it lives, but in the domain of intellectual and conscious life it is not unnatural that conscious efforts should be made toward growth and perpetuation. It is therefore natural that Christianity as the highest type of religious life should make such conscious efforts to perpetuate and expand its life creed among the peoples of the earth.

The instruments of religious growth—for since this growth is conscious and methodical it must have methods and instruments—have come to be divided under the two general heads of revival and education. Education needs hardly to be defined, but must in this case, since it is treated as a religious method, be limited to religious education. A definition of a revival is extremely difficult, for since it has so many concomitant features it is hard to determine which are essential and which are not. It may, however, be described as a periodical attempt on the part of the Church to reclaim fallen believers and gain new ones by special religious exhortations. They are designed to bring the hearer to an immediate confession of sins and profession of faith. Some revivals could find no place under this definition, but neither have they a relation to our theme. The reference is to those revivals that are brought about by special grace of the Spirit, or by a coalition of special forces in a community, quickening the religious life of the people in a most miraculous manner. They are phenomena rather than methods of growth, and have therefore no coordination with education.

A close analysis of religious education and religious revival will reveal that the revival appeals to the emotions and education to the reason of man both with the purpose of thereby influencing his will. This distinction is, however, only a general one; it cannot be denied that the revival has certain educational features, as for instance the characteristic discussion of moral precepts, or that there are emotional appeals in religious education since the presentation of great religious truths cannot leave the emotions of man unaffected. History, however, has proven the general distinction to be a correct one, notwithstanding the vigorous protest of many champions of the revival against the same.

Ordinarily the factors that enter into the revival and education are combined in the sermon. It appeals, or should appeal to all sides of man's nature. Intensified efforts, however, always make for specialization and this holds true in the religious life of the Church. With the advent of special efforts on the part of the Church to increase its membership and strengthen the faith of the members it had, the different factors of the sermon were specialized upon and separated. Special revivals and special education supplementary to the sermons were the result. In the Apostolic Church they existed coordinately as methods for furthering religious life; protracted meetings having much in common with modern revival meetings were not uncommon, while great stress was laid upon the instruction of those who became converts to the Christian cause. If they existed coordinately they did not, however, exist co-equally. Education unquestionably enjoyed the greater emphasis.

Specialization often in time leads to the elimination of one or the other thing thus separated. This was true in the history of revival and education. In the *ex opere operatum* conception of religious functions developed in the Catholic Church revivals were of course eliminated. The Reformation resurrected the revival and gave new impetus to religious education. Unfortunately, however, different denominations availed themselves of but one or the other as methods of furthering religious growth. Thus the great body of German Lutheran churches used religious education as the only means of supplementing the sermon and furthering religious growth, while those Churches that sprang up in opposition to the formalism of the semi-Catholic Church of England neglected religious education almost entirely while revivals were practically their sole strength. This development was partly due to historical factors, partly to the peculiar national characteristics of the nations mentioned. Emotionalism, in religion at least, has always appealed to the Anglo-Saxon more than to the German, whose religion has more a matter of fact nature. In America the two religious types with their characteristic methods have had the amplest opportunity to learn from one another. That opportunity has been thwarted by intolerance upon the one hand and indifference upon the other. The great body of Lutheran churches has steadily refused to recognize the revival as a dignified and efficient method of propagating Christianity, while on the other hand the clergy of the English-American churches have manifested an appalling ignorance regarding the system of catechetical instruction of the Lutheran churches.

Only a sympathetic and unprejudiced study of both methods and systems as agencies of the Church for furthering religious life can bring about a change in the attitude of both sides. The churches' duties towards the world and itself are manifold; the directions of its growth and perpetuation are different. Only in relation to these duties and the resultant function can we find a satisfactory solution of the problem.

The Church must grow inwardly and outwardly. It must seek to increase the dominance of religious precepts over the lives of its members, and it must constantly seek to gain new members, must bring others to accept religious doctrines. A third function is that of perpetuation in the exact sense of the Word. It must bring children of Christian parents to accept the faith of their fathers. This function also produces growth, both inward and outward growth, since such children are in a sense already believers, but in another sense not.

In relation to inward growth in the Church, the furthering of the great body of believers in religious precepts and in the faith of their religion, all special efforts of the Church must be supplementary to the sermon, for it has that very duty. A sermon if given forcibly and sincerely will give the religious life of the hearers nourishment and further its growth. Supplementary efforts are, however, not to be condemned. Education is obviously the most adequate in this instance. A course in religious education, such as is imparted in catechetical schools, gives a comprehensive view of the whole religious structure and a historical knowledge of the development of Christianity such as no series of sermons could impart. Many churches whose only means of such instruction is the Bible school manifest an appreciation of this fact by the emphasis they lay upon this department, aiming especially to reach the adults, not only the children.

Revivalism on the other hand is a poor method of furthering religious growth. Those factors of a revival which appeal to a mature Christian mind are to be found in a sermon. It is true that the revival does not see in this inward growth its principal purpose, but it is always considered an important secondary function. Even as such it cannot be successful. It leads to a practice of professing faith and repeating the profession at succeeding revivals, due, of course, to repeated falling from grace. These not uncommon systems of conversion and reconversion lead to instability in religious life and do little to further and intensify religious convictions.

If the revival is efficient at all, as an instrument or agency for developing religion, it ought to be in the sphere of outward growth. Few men are brought to accept Christianity by education. If they are it is not through religious education, for a person not interested in religious matters cannot be forced to study religion. Secular education has done much to prepare men for the acceptance of Christianity, but religious education can hardly be considered in this connection. Even if it has some purpose in this outward growth however, for the preparation of the newly converted for acceptance into the body of believers which is so grossly neglected by churches of the revival, it belongs in the domain of outward, not inward growth.

The revival on the other hand reaches those who would not be reached by the church service, and it not only reaches but holds them. Its characteristic discussion of moral precepts, its emphasis upon ethical questions are understood where higher religious problems would not be and the emotional appeal brings about a change in the hearer's attitude where other methods fail. There are serious questions as to the advisability of reach-

RELIGION : REVIVAL AND EDUCATION

ing the will through the emotions of man, there is cause for grave doubts as to the stability of a will thus moved; notwithstanding this fact it cannot be entirely condemned. It cannot be denied that many owe their spiritual life to such revivals, and it is a significant fact that those churches who condemn revivals unqualifiedly have never manifested very notable efforts to reach people outside of the churches' path in evangelistic mission. Even if they had they might have failed in many instances where the revival was successful, for the history of religion proves that there are many people who will never make a momentous decision, such as conversion calls for, except under the pressure of strongly moved emotions. The revival may not be the most efficient manner of winning souls, personal work seems to prove itself a better one, but it is certainly a method that has proven a degree of efficiency when its functions were not too grossly abused.

The problem of perpetuation in the narrower sense, that of raising children of Christian parentage to make an independent decision for the faith of their fathers, is clearly a problem of education. Through the parents the Church has the opportunity to impart religious instruction, and for children who are under Christian home influence, to whom religious conceptions are not entirely foreign, it is but a problem of education in these conceptions and ideas to bring them to a correct independent decision.

Churches that do not provide for such instruction sin most flagrantly against the youth. The development and increased efficiency of the Bible school marks the attempt, but an inadequate one, to rectify this error of their system. The not uncommon practice of converting children of believing parents and thus accepting them into the Church is a travesty on the Christian religion and in direct violation of the Lord's will.

The practice of accepting such children upon their maturity by a single profession of faith without knowledge of what it implies is almost equally as bad. We see therefore that education is not capable of performing all duties entrusted to the churches in addition to proclaiming the Gospel and that the revival is still less so. Many churches of America have unlimited opportunity to profit and learn from one another. May a consciousness of their own faults bring them to accept this opportunity.

[This article supplements the limited picture of Niebuhr's Yale years supplied by his own later reminiscences and the several letters written to Dr. Press which were quoted by June Bingham. It appeared in the December, 1914 number of *The Keryx*.]

3. Yale—Eden

I have been asked by the editor of *The Keryx* to write something about the life and conditions at Yale for the next number of the Keryx. I confess that, altho there is nothing that I would rather do than sing the praises of a school that has become intimately connected with my life for the past several years, I do not know just why this particular school should be of special interest to any reader of the Keryx. (I would rather like to confide to the reader that the real reason for the article is that several of the editor's high-priced stars left him in the lurch at the last moment, and rather than let the pages go blank, he thought it desirable to fill them at least with printer's ink).[1] It may be, however, that an account of Yale life will be of some interest to readers of the Keryx, first, because Yale is naturally typical of other large American universities, and secondly, because four members of our Church are at present studying in the Yale School of Religion (one is taking the Y. M. C. A. course).

Probably Yale's greatest attraction for divinity students is the fact that its school of religion is intimately connected with the whole life of the university. The school buildings are just across the street from the big campus and divinity students are eligible for practically all classes in the academical and graduate departments. In this respect Yale stands alone, the Divinity School of Chicago University being the only possible rival. Being

---

[1] The Editor of *The Keryx* for the 1914-15 school year was Helmut Richard Niebuhr.

53

thus in the very heart of one of America's greatest centers of learning gives one opportunities that are impossible in any isolated seminary. Thus, for instance, one has the privilege of hearing America's best ministers every Sunday as they come here to conduct the college services. Then, too, there are "University Lectures" every week for which the university secures eminent scholars and leaders in all fields of activity from this country and from Europe. (Those from Europe are rather scarce this year, by the way). Only last night we heard an address by David Starr Jordan, of Leland Stanford, and an authority on peace problems.

A further benefit that accrues from this close relationship with the university is the contact one may have with the large student body with its varied interests. Of course a great proportion of the "undergraduates" are sons of New York plutocrats and near-plutocrats, but there is nevertheless a large number with whom even a poor divinity student can strike up friendships, or at least acquaintances that are helpful to him in many ways. So closely is the school connected with the university that a certain former editor of the Keryx who is also studying here, considered it his duty to attend faithfully all the mass meetings that are held in every college before the big football games for the purposes of assuring the team of the school's "moral backing" by means of "organisierter Laerm". Such an ardent rooter did he become that when Yale was defeated by Harvard last week he could hardly be consoled, and is still in mourning.[2]

Regarding the School of Religion itself, I might say that in my opinion it combines scholarship and real spirituality about as ideally as this can be done. Dean Brown, head of the School, is the biggest spiritual force in Yale and he is really of great help to the many who come here and become involved in so many

---

[2] The "ardent rooter" Niebuhr referred to was Cornelius Krusé, later Professor of Philosophy at the Wesleyan University in Middletown, Connecticut.

difficult problems due to their critical studies. His talks are always a great source of inspiration. The school has in addition to daily prayers a weekly devotional meeting and also class devotional meetings, all of which are very helpful in what might otherwise be an atmosphere of cold scholarship. The professors are all very anxious to help the students personally with any problems they may have and for this reason continually invite them to dinner in order that they might cultivate a closer personal relationship with the men. I must say that I was rather surprised with the treatment I received here. I came expecting no one to take notice of my goings or comings, and I found myself in the most intimate contact with some of Yale's most famous scholars. Some of those men must make big sacrifices to put up with us and not appear to be bored.

I imagine that if any reader of the Keryx is at all interested in anything that might be said of Yale, it would be in her theology rather than in some of these aspects that I have mentioned. I will therefore defer no longer and give a somewhat general exposition of Yale's position in the theological world. Yale belongs of course to the liberal school of theological thought. There is little difference between the theology taught here and at Union Seminary. There is a widely prevalent disposition on the part of more conservative thinkers to call the theology taught here unitarian. This designation is however unjust. The general tendency of all larger American universities is of course in the general direction of unitarianism. But if this be unitarianism we may give all liberal theology that name, especially German liberal theology. Yale belongs to the "religionsgeschichtliche" school in regard to its historico-theological position. To make a very general statement about this school—it believes that Christianity need ask no quarter nor give any in its competition with other religions. It attempts to show the gradual evolution of Christian doctrines, the influences of other religions and philosophies upon them and subjects present doctrines that the Church may hold to the same historical tests. Of course it is nothing essentially new for the Church historian to animadvert upon the influences that led this or that Church father or any Christian theologian to hold the particular views which he did hold but the radicalness of liberal theology consists of its readiness to subject the canonical writings and writers to this same historical test. The result is of course that the Bible vanishes as any supernatural authority and Christianity is forced to compete with all religions upon a common basis. The truth of the Bible is for this theology true, as Spinoza so long ago contended, only because it appeals to best reason and the highest spiritual interests of men. The result of all this is that Christologies are subjected to the same criticism as any other particular doctrines, and those of Paul and John as well as those of later times. It is because of this result that Yale is accused of being unitarian. I have mentioned some of these very obvious and well-known facts about liberal theology, because I wished to explain the reason for the charge of unitarianism generally brought against the eastern schools. After the critical process has been completed the systematic theologian is left to formulate his own Christology in the light of all the facts he has at hand and his conception of Christ may be as high as even the most conservative could wish. The formulations are very different and the blanket charge of unitarianism is therefore very unjust tho it must be confessed that for him who does care to draw fine distinctions the general tendency to reject the preexistence of Christ is unitarianism without more ado.

I will let this very meager description of Yale thought suffice. If one of the Yale professors should see it, it would probably make his hair stand on end. I have busied myself while here more with philosophy of religion than with theology and tho my competence is not great in either field, I feel myself especially insecure upon the latter field.

It might be of some interest to the readers to know that German influence is naturally very great here. In the classes one hears nothing but German names referred to: Holtzman, Weizsaecker, Weinel, Gunkel, Weiss, Deissman, Dobschuetz and all of the rest of the tribe are constantly passing in review. Prof. Bacon, probably the best known Yale theologian is a great admirer of German scholarship and holds degrees from five German universities. One of the pleasing things for us has been, that altho we are somewhat ostracized for not holding any academical degree we have found this somewhat compensated for by the fact that we speak and read German. We often find ourselves called upon to review German books not yet translated.

This constant demand for original research in the sources themselves is by the way one of the most helpful things at Yale. Of course that is not particularly unique of Yale, but it was rather new to me. In the course of a year one is required to wade thru an endless number of books and this first-hand knowledge of prominent writers is more educative than any of the classroom work. One is not expected to take more than fourteen hours a week, but the required reading keeps one more than busy. I am glad that a great deal of progress has been made at Eden in amassing a library so that this sort of study will become more and more possible. I am ashamed to remember that I had barely a speaking acquaintance with the library there.

I cannot forgo this opportunity without saying a word regarding the position we were placed in here because of the fact that we had no academical degree, a matter to which I have already alluded. Yale is at present the only school of any standing that will at all consider giving a man a degree if he does not possess the A. B. That is one very good reason for coming to Yale. But the dean has told me that Yale will be forced to apply more stringent rules in the future simply to protect its academical standing, and study here will therefore become increasingly difficult.

A man without a degree is, for the first year at least, under constant difficulty and in continual embarrassment. It is for this reason that I have lost no opportunity and will lose none to express the hope that it will soon be possible for our Church to arrange a college course that will receive full credit in the academical world. Even the Mennonites come here with an A. B. and take their place among the chosen while we are forced to look on naked of those garments without which a man is considered a barbarian in the academical world.[3]

---

[3] As some of the later writings in this collection show, Niebuhr considered the absence of degrees at Elmhurst and Eden a major deficiency.

[On October 15, 1915, the German Evangelical Synod of North America celebrated its 75th anniversary. Niebuhr preached at Bethel Church twice that day, once in German and once in English, and both of his sermons (which have survived in manuscript form) are included here.]

4. An Anniversary Sermon[1]

We celebrate today, as you know, the 75th anniversary of our Church. Actually, our Synod had a double origin. The first origin of the Evangelical Church took place in Prussia in the year 1817. It was there that the Evangelical principle of the union was born. It was from there, then, that it was spread by immigrants from the old Fatherland. Perhaps it would be interesting to say a few things about the Evangelical Principle. The Evangelical Church came into being in 1817 when it occurred to the King of Prussia that there was really no essential difference between the Lutheran and Reformed Churches. As you know, Luther and Calvin were the principal reformers. The one founded the Lutheran and the other the Reformed Church. Zwingli however, was actually the first Reformed theologian. Yet he was prematurely called away from his work. As some of you still know, the two parties fought in particular about a point concerning the doctrine of the Lord's Supper. Various worldly princes tried to smooth out the differences, and from the Reformation on, people were ready to declare the differences insignificant. But when Zwingli, in a public discussion, offered Luther the hand of brotherhood, the latter refused it roughly in the sincere opinion that the Zwinglian interpretation of the Lord's Supper was not biblical. The result was a

---

[1]The following Sermon has been translated from the German by Catherine Keller, to whom I am greatly indebted.

conflict which lasted for centuries, until the time of William the Third, who like many others was convinced that the Christian Church in Germany should not be so divided. He named a committee to draw up an agenda by which both parties would meet on common ground. This took place, and so the Prussian *Landeskirche* was born. Naturally, many who took part in the great migrations of the 19th Century subscribed to this principle. Thus, the Prussian Evangelical Church now had a shoot in the New World like all the other church groups of Europe.

Our Synod started small, of course, smaller than the rest. First just six pastors joined together with their congregations; for a long time growth was very small. But then the Synod began to unite with other church groups. Institutions were built for the education of preachers. Home missions were carried out by which many souls were won for the Synod. Finally, the mission to the pagans was begun and carried on with the appropriate zeal. Now we are so far along that we perform all of the responsibilities of an independent church body. The Synod can now count over a thousand pastors and over thirteen hundred congregations. The Lord has visibly blessed our work. We do not, however, wish to maintain that He loves us more than other churches and that we are more pleasing to Him. The Synod, on the contrary, was built upon the principle of unity. We do not believe that we are the only church which saves. The truth is many-sided, even Christian truth, and it is granted to one church as it is one people to especially see one side, and another to see another side.

Nonetheless God has shown us mercy. We have been able to develop peacefully, we have been able to worship our God in the manner to which we were accustomed in our Fatherland. He has visibly manifested his grace in us. We are certainly a strong church today, and though we cannot perhaps be reckoned among the strongest, we have nonetheless developed a

AN ANNIVERSARY SERMON

power that enables us to exercise an influence on the life of the people which is by no means minimal.

God has shown us grace, we say first of all, because we have been allowed to develop according to our gifts and our abilities. The German character, like every other, has its unique traits. And our Church is especially suited to the German character. It is God's grace that we have been able to develop according to our own individuality and to discover our God in the way we learned from our fathers.

First we ought to mention in this connection that seriousness is peculiar to the German character. German religion is not as emotional as some others. For this reason it is not expected that we come to Christianity by way of a sudden upheaval of our world of feelings as is the case in certain other American religions. We naturally grow up as Christians. Through Confirmation instruction we are educated to the principles of Christianity. Perhaps there is a danger that seriousness turns to indifference. I am convinced that such a danger exists. But that is not our concern at present.

Yet another trait of the German character, one which has become especially famous in recent times, is *Gruendlichkeit*—thoroughness. And the German has attempted to be thorough in religion as well as in everything else. Thus, German Christianity has proved itself very intelligent and very active. I don't know if it is always as intelligent and active as in the Old World. But it ought to be.

Certain characteristics are hard to pinpoint precisely. We do have all of our prejudices and customs and traditions, and we have been able to worship our God according to them and to the faith of our fathers.

However, the grace which has been shown to us as a church and as people should not be carried off like spoils. The grace of God should not be in vain for us. We should become fellow workers, as Paul says. If we have had the grace that let us develop in our religious life according to our unique traits, so also we have the duty to serve with our unique gifts. The German spirit certainly does have characteristics that one does not otherwise find so sharply defined. And we have the duty to dedicate these special gifts to the culture and the religious life of this country. This is especially desirable in view of the fact that this nation is made up of all the peoples of the world and can only develop itself rightly when all of them sacrifice their best on the altar of their nation. To do this, we must show a lively interest in the Christian development of this country. We cannot be satisfied to worship our God just for ourselves off in some corner. We must serve Him with our special strength. In this respect I believe we have left much to be desired in the past. We are indeed small, but we haven't exercised as great an influence as we could have according to our size. We should represent a noteworthy force in the religious life of our people. For example, the principle of confirmation is one that has met with a great deal of approval in this country and always finds entrance into American churches. Our Christian celebrations, especially Good Friday, have found much sympathy among Americans, who had formerly never quite learned how to celebrate such holidays. In certain other respects we have exercised an influence—but it could and must become much greater.

To work correctly it is also necessary to take from others where we lack, as we attempt to give where others lack. Thus, even in our Christian life we can learn much from our neighbors. In this also we see that grace is not given us in vain. Let us consider for a moment what an opportunity is thus presented to us in this country. The Christian peoples of all nations have gathered together here. They have each brought along their unique shaping of Christianity. Some have false ideas to which was wanted neither in heaven or in hell. So it may be that there are churches that have no real individuality. Every church ought to stand for something definite and be a definite force in the community. Personality and individuality cannot be bequeathed. The struggles of the fathers of our church, their ideas and their convictions, are not ours except if we make them so. We must develop an individuality as a church.

There are several things our church stands for now. It stands for the spirit of common sense in religion. Evangelical Christianity has never attempted to be sensational nor tried to find converts through some special emotional stress. It has never adopted artificial means of propagating faith. It has rather believed that education was the most potent of factors of Christian growth: The Sunday School and the Confirmation Class. One method is particularly our own and the other we have learned from our neighbors.[3] We did well both to learn from others and to retain the approved methods which we ourselves had. We have by this made Christian education particularly potent in religious life. Sometimes we fret because public schools have consistently refused to instruct in religion. We ought to do less fretting and work more diligently that the church may do what seems impossible for a state to do in order that it may preserve its principle of separation of church and state.

Our church furthermore stands for a continual emphasis on the spiritual as a source of the moral. We are particularly anxious that the spiritual wells from which all true morality springs even run fresh. In this we are not alone but we insist on this with particular emphasis. These are some elements of our individuality.

---

[3]The Evangelical Synod was particularly strong in catechetical instruction from its beginning. Indeed, a distinctive *Evangelischer Katechismus* appeared as early as 1847 and continues to be used in churches of the Evangelical tradition in a revised form even to this day.

We hardly need more but we need to emphasize them with greater force. There are many personalities in this world who believe the right and do the right, but they do not work with sufficient force. As a church we ought to try to be a forceful personality, one that has to be counted within the Christian forces of this country and the Christian forces that go to make up the kingdom of God.

Strong individuality does not need to be in competition with other individuals. The artist does not compete with the scientist or the scientist with the poet. The man who acts does not compete with the man who thinks, the man who leads with the man who can readily follow. All put in their share that the whole may be strong.

A nation is a unity because individuals of many kinds with many ideals, with different temperaments, with various powers, all lay their particular gifts upon the altar of their country. Their common purpose alone makes the nation one. The nation is not a unity because of the uniformity of its citizens. The kingdom of God and the Christian Church will not achieve unity because of the uniformity of belief or action. Each church and each Christian can retain his individuality. We need not be in competition either. We achieve unity because of our common purpose to bring about the coming of the kingdom of God. This purpose ought to be a holy zeal and the earnestness of our task ought to bring us together to work for a common end, though with different methods and various powers. Our highest ambition as a church ought to be that we may be an integral part of the church that serves its master, an integral power by serving him according to the light God has given us to see the light.

we cannot subscribe. Others possess something that belongs to a living Christianity. Thus, for example, the development of the Christian Sunday School is something utterly American. In Germany religious instruction in the schools renders this less necessary. But no matter what we do, we will not be able to keep up such instruction in the public schools. For this reason the development of the Sunday School is especially necessary. We have proved ourselves ready to learn in this respect, and our Sunday Schools are now, I believe, as thorough and as well attended as any.

The social development of the congregation is also strictly American. Our many clubs for young and old should not be viewed as a kind of defamation of the holy purpose of the church but as a development necessary in this country.

We have lived for 75 years as a church in this country. We look back and thank God for His grace in allowing us to develop according to the faith of our fathers. As often as we look backwards with thanksgiving, however, we must also look ahead for new tasks in order to express our thanks with more than words. What could be more natural than to use our unique strengths for the good of our nation and to work for the victory of God's kingdom as an expression of gratitude for being allowed to grow in accordance with our individuality. If we want to do it as a church, we must also lead genuinely Christian lives as individuals, sympathetic to our country.

5. That They May All Be One

We are today celebrating the diamond anniversary of our church. As I have already done I shall give a short explanation of the history and significant events in our church. Really, our particular church was founded in this country 75 years ago. But the principles which have given it strength and purpose are older. They date back about a hundred years and have their roots in Germany. At that time Germany was divided into two camps, the Reformed and Lutheran. A good king thought the differences which separated them did not warrant their separation and under his influence they were amalgamated into the Evangelical Church, to this day the State Church of Germany. We were founded upon the principle of union. Therefore and for this reason our church has the motto which I have chosen for our text.[1] I think it would be appropriate to speak upon the principle of Christian unity upon the occasion of this anniversary. I believe there will be a day when all Christendom will be one. It was the expressed wish of our Lord. For that reason also it ought to be our devout endeavor. But there are other practical reasons why we ought to dare to hope that some day the Christian forces will be united.

In the first place denominationalism is a perpetuation of historical differences, many of which have no real value in the present day. I have mentioned the historical setting of our own church. Every church has such history and cherishes it. Now it

---

[1] The text for Niebuhr's sermon was John 17:21. The sermon itself is without a title, but the words from the text, "That they may all be one," certainly represent its intent.

is not necessary to fly into the teeth of the past and to declare all historical tradition as non-important. Our fathers did not work and think in vain. Many precious grains of truth they winnowed from the chaff for our benefit. Nevertheless there are some things that our fathers believed that have no authority over us, and there are some things they did which would be less well for us to do. Progress is continually being made and new situations come up which we must meet. For this reason we ought not let the historical situations of the past dominate us today. We also have our particular problems and we ought to meet them as best we may. Times bring great changes. Our fathers met them and so ought we. We ought not allow the forces of the past to drive us into the future.

In the second place, most of the denominational differences are not essential. There is really hardly an essential difference of doctrine between the churches of the Reformation. They are mostly differences of temperament. The one emphasizes one aspect of Christianity more and the other some other aspect. The Calvinist emphasizes the sovereignty of God and the Methodist the freedom of man. The Reformed makes the sermon the central force of the worship and the Lutheran the sacrament. The truth is so many-sided and not one of us is able to grasp it completely. We ought to be tolerant with people who see the truth a little differently than we do and who worship with slightly different forms. Of course there are some important differences, but really they are not so much between the denominations as they are in them themselves. There are wider differences between Evangelical and Evangelical than there are between Lutheran and Evangelical or Evangelical and Reformed. The differences between us are mostly differences of church government, of temperament and of history.[2]

---

[2] Niebuhr's reaction to the broad diversity in his own denomination was elaborated in a letter to Dr. Press dated November 3, 1915. He found the

In the third place we ought to get together because Christianity in dead earnest will not brook the division of forces caused by denominationalism. Christianity is more in dead earnest in the mission field than any other place. There it stands on the firing line and therefore it has no time for petty divisions, just as all parties in a nation blend into one patriotic whole when the time comes to advance to the firing line. As far as denominationalism goes, missionaries are the most liberal of all ministers and least concerned with the petty denominational differences that separate them. One reason that we can exist with such a division of forces in this country and in others is that we are not earnest enough in our prayer that the kingdom might come, for a kingdom divided against itself must fall and therefore certainly cannot come into its full power and glory.

But before there will be any union, and you and I will not see it completed, there must be the greatest possible development of individuality. Churches have individuality just as persons have. Just as each person brings something to the community by his own peculiar individuality so the churches add something to the kingdom of God by the particular contribution which they make. We are celebrating today the anniversary of a church. We ought therefore speak not so much of the dissolution of that church ultimately in one great body of the Christian Church as of the development of its own individuality so that it will have something to contribute to the whole.

There are some individuals with little individuality. Kipling tells the story of Tomlison who had so little personality that he

---

"laughable medieval theories" of some of his fellow pastors made him "both angry and despondent." "They continually awake the suspicion in me that the forces of reaction in our church are much stronger than the progressives, so strong that no great hope for betterment is in sight. To be very candid with you I do not feel at all at home in our church. I do not know whether Yale is the cause of this. I hope that I would have had enough sense without Yale influence to resent the imbecile standpatism of some sections of our church."

was wanted neither in heaven or in hell. So it may be that there are churches that have no real individuality. Every church ought to stand for something definite and be a definite force in the community. Personality and individuality cannot be bequeathed. The struggles of the fathers of our church, their ideas and their convictions, are not ours except if we make them so. We must develop an individuality as a church.

There are several things our church stands for now. It stands for the spirit of common sense in religion. Evangelical Christianity has never attempted to be sensational nor tried to find converts through some special emotional stress. It has never adopted artificial means of propagating faith. It has rather believed that education was the most potent of factors of Christian growth: The Sunday School and the Confirmation Class. One method is particularly our own and the other we have learned from our neighbors.[3] We did well both to learn from others and to retain the approved methods which we ourselves had. We have by this made Christian education particularly potent in religious life. Sometimes we fret because public schools have consistently refused to instruct in religion. We ought to do less fretting and work more diligently that the church may do what seems impossible for a state to do in order that it may preserve its principle of separation of church and state.

Our church furthermore stands for a continual emphasis on the spiritual as a source of the moral. We are particularly anxious that the spiritual wells from which all true morality springs even run fresh. In this we are not alone but we insist on this with particular emphasis. These are some elements of our individuality.

---

[3]The Evangelical Synod was particularly strong in catechetical instruction from its beginning. Indeed, a distinctive *Evangelischer Katechismus* appeared as early as 1847 and continues to be used in churches of the Evangelical tradition in a revised form even to this day.

We hardly need more but we need to emphasize them with greater force. There are many personalities in this world who believe the right and do the right, but they do not work with sufficient force. As a church we ought to try to be a forceful personality, one that has to be counted within the Christian forces of this country and the Christian forces that go to make up the kingdom of God.

Strong individuality does not need to be in competition with other individuals. The artist does not compete with the scientist or the scientist with the poet. The man who acts does not compete with the man who thinks, the man who leads with the man who can readily follow. All put in their share that the whole may be strong.

A nation is a unity because individuals of many kinds with many ideals, with different temperaments, with various powers, all lay their particular gifts upon the altar of their country. Their common purpose alone makes the nation one. The nation is not a unity because of the uniformity of its citizens. The kingdom of God and the Christian Church will not achieve unity because of the uniformity of belief or action. Each church and each Christian can retain his individuality. We need not be in competition either. We achieve unity because of our common purpose to bring about the coming of the kingdom of God. This purpose ought to be a holy zeal and the earnestness of our task ought to bring us together to work for a common end, though with different methods and various powers. Our highest ambition as a church ought to be that we may be an integral part of the church that serves its master, an integral power by serving him according to the light God has given us to see the light.

[On October 31, 1915, Bethel Evangelical Church celebrated Reformation Sunday. In German, Niebuhr delivered the following didactic tribute to the Reformation, stressing the need for its continuation.]

6. A Reformationsfest Sermon

Today a large part of the Protestant Church is celebrating Reformation Day. On this day we think about the event in world history which took place four hundred years ago. There are holidays that celebrate events that had meaning only for a small portion of the world. For example, the world does not participate when the Mexicans celebrate their Independence Day, because the world cannot enjoy the freedom that reigns there. Thus one might also suspect Protestantism of exaggerating beyond any truth the importance of the event. But no, on this point worldly historians agree with us. There is no history in which the Reformation is not as fully handled as for example, the fall of the Roman Empire, as the 50-year war or as our Revolution. Historically one reckons the so-called modern time (*Neuzeit*) from the Reformation on. At that point the Middle Ages — with its chaos in government, its lack of education among the people, and its general superstitiousness — came to a close. With the Reformation, humanity begins a new epoch which we can indeed call the period of maturity, for with the Reformation childish superstition was surrendered and an enlightened faith became the object of life.

Thus we cannot overestimate the meaning of the Reformation. Almost all the modern views of life that have become flesh and blood for us — so much so that we don't even realize that they are modern and new — stem directly or indirectly from the Reformation. The hero of this time, Martin Luther, belongs for this reason among the unquestionable greats of history. Counted in terms of sheer importance, the name of this great man must be written next to the name of a Caesar and a Frederick the Great, a Lincoln and a Gladstone.

It is therefore an important historical event that we consider today, and we rejoice that as Protestants we were especially influenced by the Reformation and possess its special blessing. Thus we are looking back into the past at ourselves. And yet for this reason we also are in danger of propping ourselves up on the past. We are in danger of boasting that we are Protestants, that we undid the superstition that reigns in the Roman Church, that we are the ones that stand especially near to God in grace.

I would like to address this danger today and point out that however great the influence of a great personality and a great event may have been on the world, we do not automatically inherit its blessing. No spiritual goods can be automatically bequeathed or inherited. The word of the poet remains eternally true:

> "That which you have inherited from your fathers
> you must win in order to possess."

This quote rather than a Bible verse came to me out of the blue as a brief summary of that which we want to consider together today. But our text expresses the same thought.[1] The Jews are also propping themselves up on the past. They wanted to live from what Abraham had earned. "We have Abraham as our father," was the way they wanted to express their privileged position in the kingdom of God. We have the Reformation as our father. We are the children of its blessing. Yet neither Abraham nor the Reformation can become a blessing for us if

---

[1] Unfortunately, the text employed in the service is unknown.

A REFORMATIONSFEST SERMON

we do not continually learn anew the lessons that they taught. Their spiritual gifts do not let themselves be inherited. They must be won in the sweat of our brow. Certainly, the past has shown us the way. But we must pioneer the way ourselves.

Let us apply this to several of the Reformation's blessings.

First, the Reformation means for us the rediscovery of the principle of justification by faith. Humanity was groaning under the church-righteousness of the Roman Church. Holiness had to be earned through ecclesiastical actions, penance, fasts, masses, sacrifice, indulgences and so forth. Luther read the writings of a man who, like himself, had to fight against the unrighteousness of the law, the Apostle Paul's letter to the Romans, and it became suddenly clear to him, "Man is not justified by the works of the law but by faith alone." These were the words which were written on the banner of the new movement. And these are the words that we now repeat after the Reformation and the Apostle Paul. But we are not justified because we know that we are justified by faith. We are not yet justified because we know the truth, but we become righteous when we live the truth. And let it be said here that the faith which justifies is not merely assent to all that the Church or even Holy Scripture says. Neither is faith a lukewarm acceptance of the fact that there is a heaven and eternity and a God. God does not repay us with holiness for our recognition of Him. This is the greatest mistake which the Reformation sought to correct — holiness was seen as a kind of reward for the faithful. The faith which justifies is indeed more than faith. Paul understood by this concept an inner prayer-relationship with God. He wanted to say that prayer, the essence of morality, is the root of righteousness. He knew that one who is internally bound to God has a power that does not belong to others. The faith of a Paul was not a weak assent to the facts of a general world religion. It was a relation of friendship with God. And

71

this is the sole faith by which we become righteous. The Reformation did not rescue us from superstition. We must rescue us from superstition. We must rescue ourselves. We must believe for ourselves and ourselves stand in fellowship with God.

A second principle of the Reformation is the priesthood of all believers. Before the Reformation, the individual Christian had to be dependent upon the priest and the Church for his fellowship with God. The Church mediated. Her sacraments freed one from sin. Her absolution bestowed grace. Her laws expressed the will of God. Outside of the Church no holiness could be found.

Protestantism taught, however, that no one stands between God and the human soul which seeks Him. He can reveal His will to us when we seek it; He can forgive our sins when we come to Him in humility, and sincerely pray, "God be merciful to me, a sinner." The Saints, the Christians, are all priests; they can all pray to God, they can all hear His voice.

This right is a great blessing. Humanity always possessed it, but it is also a blessing that we again become conscious of the nobility that we lost. But this is a blessing which we must win if we would own it. So you yourself pray to your God, or do you just participate in the Church? Have you already been driven to prayer by a straightforward recognition of your guilt or do you just speak the confession of sin in Church? Have you already spent hours in communion with your God and have you in those hours won a new joy of living and a new certainty that you are with God in grace? If not, then Luther labored in vain and Huss died pointlessly. The Reformation had served no purpose for you.

I would like to call attention to yet a third principle of the Reformation. It is that of the holiness of all vocations. Under Catholicism we cannot attain to the highest blessedness in just

A REFORMATIONSFEST SERMON

any profession. The priest and the monk and the nun rank higher than the simple Christian. The result of this teaching was that during the Middle Ages the land was overrun by monks and friars who could not exist without taxes, often at the expense of the simple folk. There is also something noble about the orders of the Catholic Church, and much that is worthy of imitation. But the principle which justifies their existence is fundamentally false.

We do not have to lock ourselves up behind monastery walls when we wish to attain holiness. We can do our duty in our vocations. The mother who teaches her children godliness has a more holy vocation than a nun. The man who is honest in his business and mixes authority with Christian love towards his employees serves his God. But our profession is not in and of itself holy. It is not unholy, but neither is it necessarily holy. We must hallow it, hallow it through holy motives, through the spirit of love, through Christian justice. People should recognize us in our business life as Christians. People should find a Christian uniqueness in our professional life. I honor the monk and the nun, for they seek something better than average righteousness. But I feel sorry for them, for they have set out upon the wrong path. The right way has been shown us. But we don't follow it. And if not, then the Reformation has been for naught. So it is with its spiritual gifts: we must win them if we wish to possess them. It is true that the past rains blessings upon us, that martyrs died for us, but their sacrifice is in vain when we do not follow where they lead. Indeed, even the greatest of all martyrs died for us in vain if we do not follow Him. His death is not a magical power which makes us holy. Let us heed his own Word: "Whoever would be my disciple, let him take up his cross and follow me."

[This was the first of a number of pieces Niebuhr wrote on Christian Education themes for *The Evangelical Teacher*, appearing in the May, 1916 issue. From January 1917 until February, 1918 he was its Associate Editor.]

7. The Scylla and Charybdis of Teaching

The ancient Homeric legend of Scylla and Charybdis, the two great cliffs where sea monsters dwelt, and between which Ulysses had to sail, is generally familiar. There is a Scylla and Charybdis in almost every undertaking, two opposite dangers, two extremes, between which one must sail and both of which one must avoid if the undertaking is to be successful. In Sunday-school instruction the Scylla is the temptation to teach religious and Biblical history for its own sake and the Charybdis is the temptation to use the lessons purely as texts for the inculcation of moral and spiritual truths. Some Sunday-school teachers suffer shipwreck on Scylla and others founder on Charybdis and all of us have an anxious time steering between the two.

Originally Sunday-school instruction was meant merely to give a comprehensive and exhaustive knowledge of Biblical history. Its purpose was believed to be accomplished if the pupil could recite the names of all the kings who presided over the fortunes of Israel, could give the dates of the principal historical events, could trace the missionary journeys of Paul and was able to give sundry other information on the history of Old Testament peoples and the New Testament church. The "International Uniform" lessons were designed with the avowed purpose of teaching the scholar the whole of bibical history. Chronological sequence, rather than pedagogical usefulness, was the determining principle in the choice of lessons. The result was that many lessons of doubtful pedagogical value were used, and that Christian scholars were forced to take their spiritual sustenance principally from Old Testament lessons. For no other reason but

THE SCYLLA AND CHARYBDIS OF TEACHING

that the Old Testament is larger than the New, two lessons were presented out of the Old Testament to every one out of the New Testament. This weakness in the International Uniform system has been somewhat remedied, but never entirely overcome, in late years. It has been as much the cause of the modern revolt against the International Uniform lessons as the ascendency of the principle of grading.

If Sunday-school teachers have been prone to stay too closely with the historical element in the lesson, it has, for this reason, not been entirely their fault. The material which they used must bear part of the blame. But even with the best possible lesson material there is an ever present temptation to teach history for its own sake. Not infrequently we hear teachers burdening their pupils with the minutest details in the historical part of the lesson, and insisting on exact knowledge regarding every geographical and historical element in the lesson. It is unnecessary to say that a fair knowledge of the geographical and historical background of the lesson adds to its interest. But sometimes the background is painted with such vivid detail that it obscures the characters and movements that ought to dominate the scene. The tendency to do this seems to be more a matter of wrong principle than of wrong methods. It is based upon the principle that the influence of the Bible is more or less automatic, that, therefore, an intimate acquaintance with its entire contents will have a salutary effect on the pupil's character.

Now the Bible is history, religious and spiritual history, and history is always a good teacher. But for most people, especially for the young, it needs retouching. It is too photographic. Photography seldom teaches anything. It is too much a slave to detail. To teach lessons and present messages is the business of art, of the art of the painter, for instance. He can take the same subject that the photographer has used and retouch it, make the salient features stand out and not only a story is told, but a message is given. The business of the teacher must conform to that the artist rather than to that of the photographer. Of course, just as the power of the artist is in the subject he chooses, as well as the way in which he treats his subject, so the pedagogical power of history is to be found in the choice of lessons, as well as in the way an individual lesson is treated. The individual teacher has no voice in the selection of the lesson texts, but every teacher can put those touches on a lesson that make the characters live and the story fruitful of moral inspiration.

There are some teachers who are so afraid of foundering on the Scylla of history that they steer too closely to Charybdis. They extract a moral out of their lesson and then treat their lesson with the same scant courtesy that ministers are alleged to accord their texts. The reason this is an ineffective method of teaching is that abstractions do not arouse the interest of a child. It resents as an insult to its intelligence the effort of the teacher to explain that "this story teaches us that we must be, etc." It does not resent it explicitly, but its reaction to the lesson is equivalent to that. Of course, the child likes its morals fairly obvious. It doesn't mind if we say that David was courageous in killing the giant, or if we describe his confidence in God, if we dwell upon Joseph's readiness to forgive his brothers or his devotion to his father, but it is willing to dispense with the explanation that these characters teach us that we "ought to be courageous, confident, forgiving and loving." The child will draw the morals for its own life if the story is only clear cut enough to have a moral. The natural development of the child is by imitation, and it will unconsciously resolve to emulate the example of some captivating personality if the personality is appealingly presented. The child does not want its lessons embalmed in moral precepts. It wants the truth as it lives in history and in people.

THE SCYLLA AND CHARYBDIS OF TEACHING

As has been indicated before, the attempt of the teacher to steer between Scylla and Charybdis is often complicated by the choice of lessons. Some historical material is so poorly adapted for pedagogical use that the teacher is forced either to treat it merely as history or to extract some lesson that the text is alleged to teach, and then turn his back resolutely upon the text for fear that the pupil will discover that it fails to teach the lesson convincingly. But this weakness is being gradually overcome in all lesson systems and more and more attention is being paid to pedagogical availability. This is the reason why "extra-Biblical" history is being increasingly employed. This opens up a new wealth of material and therefore offers a wider latitude in choosing lessons that have pedagogical value.

But very often this tendency in modern Sunday-school work founders very badly on what we have chosen to call Charybdis. It offers the pupil a dry assortment of moral precepts that never will arrest his interest. If the tendency to use extra-Biblical material remains in the historical field, however, it seems destined to succeed ultimately, though it has many difficulties to overcome. But whether the pedagogical principle in the choice of lessons becomes more exacting because of greater freedom in the choice of lessons or not, there is no question but that it must continue to become more exacting. The only history that teaches anything is the history that presents definite issues and distinctive and unique personalities. The incidents must, in other words, have a dramatic element and the characters must be, to put it somewhat bluntly, either heroes or villains. Not all characters of history are distinctive, not all the personalities of Biblical lore are either heroes or villains. The attempts of some lesson expounders to make heroes out of characters with little of the heroic in them, or villains out of men whose villainy was not convincing, often produce a sense of unreality in the pupil who reads them.

But whatever may be the difficulties both of Sunday-school teachers and those who arrange its lessons, the ideal of both must be to teach spiritual and moral truths by means of moral and spiritual history. There are schools where history may be taught for its own sake and moral precepts inculcated independently of history, but for the Sunday-school these two methods are dangers to be avoided.

["The Future of Our Seminaries," appeared in February, 1917 and took advantage of *The Keryx's* wide readership beyond the Seminary. Again Niebuhr broached the question of modernizing the Synod's educational institutions that he earlier raised in "Yale—Eden."]

8. The Future of Our Seminaries

As I understand it *The Keryx* was created to serve a larger purpose than that of the usual college paper. The average college paper, with a clientel largely comprised of the student body, is satisfied to entertain its readers with more or less personal news which incidentally is generally also more or less facetious. *The Keryx* was born to a serious purpose. Its founders conceived its duty to be the arousing of interest in our schools and thru this interest to work for higher standards. To this duty *The Keryx* has, in the main, been true and its influence for good, I believe, has not been inconsiderable. Of course *The Keryx* can not be a propaganda magazine. The writer well remembers several letters he received during his brief reign over its destinies which very pointedly inquired whether the students thought that they ought to instruct the ministers. Nevertheless *The Keryx* has indirectly contributed a great deal to better our schools by awakening and maintaining interest in them.

Friendly interest incites love and love can work wonders. But interest also reveals defects which love strives to correct. We all love the schools which harbored us for years and were in many respects our intellectual and spiritual mothers. One does not easily criticize mothers. It seems blasphemous. But, in this case at least, love is maintained for the mothers not only by the thought of what they were to us but of what they might be. Our schools are not perfect. No schools are but it will not harm us to be candid and admit that the imperfections of our seminaries are more serious than those which even the best schools are willing to acknowledge, even as saints penitently confess their sins. There is nothing the matter with the spiritual character of our schools. The writer does not think the spiritual atmosphere to have been bad in his day. He must acknowledge a spiritual debt to many men with whom he came in contact there both among students and professors. The faults, as they are, are purely academic.

To begin with the work of our schools does not conform to the standards set all about us. It is a well-known fact that a minister in this country is expected to have an eleven-year education. He ought to be a graduate of high school, college, and theological seminary. He ought to have the degrees of A. B. and B. D., not for the sake of the degrees themselves, but for the sake of the academical achievement which they indicate. However frantically our schools may have been trying to crowd the equivalent of eleven years of study into seven or even eight years, they have not succeeded and never can. Pure mathematics is against them. Within their limitations they have done work of which we may all be proud. But they can not accomplish the impossible. In other words we need a college, not a junior college but a fully accredited one. This is not a new thought or new ideal. But it is one of which we can not too frequently be reminded. It is not necessary to dwell upon the changes that would be necessary to realize this ideal. For one thing about twice as many professors would be needed in both schools. Other, perhaps even more important changes are obviously necessary but need not be enumerated. Why should we enumerate changes that can not be accomplished? But why can they not be accomplished? The answer is ready. Finances will not permit. It is easy for the writer and others to speak of ideals when they have not been forced to deal with the hard cold facts

THE FUTURE OF OUR SEMINARIES

of reality as some valiant gentlemen who preside over the destinies of our school have. These men have the same ideals and, unlike the writer, they have really tried to realize them. But everywhere they have been thwarted by the indifference of the churches. So the problem does resolve itself to a matter of interest after all. If our Church ever makes up its mind to want first-class educational institutions really badly it will be able to get them.

But the financial problem is also one of method. The writer has the temerity of all amateurs and bleacherites to offer suggestions to the managers. Here is the first one. Students ought to pay more for their education. How easy it is to say this after one is safely thru. None of us realized the "snap" we had while we were at school. We never had to worry about bed or breakfast or any other meal and not one of us, even those who paid in full, really paid enough to cover their board. If our seminaries would not charge a cent tuition and simply held the students responsible for their board they would be better off than they are now. They are about the only schools in America that hold themselves responsible for the board of the students. Perhaps the custom is a relic of the days of the "Missionshaus," when the students raised their own potatoes and the school was forced to pay $2.00 a bushel for them. But what about those who can not afford to pay for their board? Ought they therefore be deprived of an education? Poverty among students is not confined to our schools. Men are working their way thru schools where it costs four times as much as at our seminaries. Of course these schools do not leave their students to shift absolutely for themselves. They offer scholarships to the worthy ones. We could do that too. Scholarships from different congregations to be known under the name of the congregation would on the one hand encourage financial support from our congregations and on the other restrict the largest of our institutions to those alone who are worthy of it.

Another thing might be said of the financial problem, not of the present, but of the future. If we ever have a college, that will not mean that three or four years will have to be added to the present terms of our schools. It will mean that three or four years ought to be pushed off at the bottom. The Church ought not be responsible for the high school education of its youths. That they can get at home. In other words, it ought to demand a high school diploma of its Elmhurst men. We have a far way to go until all this is realized and some obstacles seem insurmountable. When we think of these things we are liable to say discouragedly:

"So many worlds, so much to do,
So little done, such things to be."

But after all our goal is a necessary one and therefore it must also be a possible one. And if we realize it to be necessary we will make it possible.

We want fully accredited schools not for the degrees they give with which we might lift ourselves upon terms of equality with our American brethren. Even that is not an ignoble desire. One tires of being an academical outcast in a profession in which academical standards are so persistently applied. But above all we do want fully accredited schools for the education behind their degrees. We may have a fairly adequate professional training but we lack the foundation of a general education. Since the day of the writer our schools have improved considerably and if he enumerates his deficiencies they may not fit the present situation, but even now we can hardly term our general education adequate. In an age of science we know little about the higher sciences. In a day which brings practically every religious problem into some relation to the doctrine of

THE FUTURE OF OUR SEMINARIES

evolution we left school, knowing no more about this bugaboo of theology, "evolution," than the mere word. Our knowledge of psychology and philosophy was snatched on "quick lunch" counters and we had no time to make a thorough study of sociology while everyone about us was speaking about the "social gospel." The history we learned was no more than any high school boy learns and we were high school boys when we learned it. We learned the dates and the names of history's heroes but we had no understanding of its profounder meanings and no appreciation for its lessons. If there is any deficiency which the writer feels particularly it is his lack of historical knowledge. A minister ought to know history well not only because it is a fund for illustrative material but because it helps us to appraise our own day and age and to understand the "signs of the times."

There is a great store of knowledge that we ought to have but do not have. We will have to do the best we can to acquire it by personal study but for those who come after us we covet a better preparation for a calling that ought to have nothing but the best.

["A Modern Sunday School," revealed Niebuhr's concern for the Sunday school program, growing out of an awareness that progress may not itself represent improvement. It was published in the October, 1917 issue of *The Evangelical Teacher*.]

9. A Modern Sunday School

No one likes to be old fashioned. Speak of something as modern, and you generally commend it to sympathetic attention. Most of us want modern Sunday schools. We want to keep abreast of the progress. But sometimes the vanguard of progress moves so swiftly that it is difficult to keep pace. That is particularly true of Sunday school progress. It has been astoundingly rapid. The reason for the rapidity of its development is that religious education was forced not only to overtake secular educational standards, which had a much earlier development, but to keep abreast of them also, for secular education was not remaining stationary while religious education was attempting to overtake it. The rapidity of this progress was accentuated in our own church because we took our first steps somewhat belatedly and were just discarding the "Fibel" for the Uniform lessons of the Bible when the movement to displace Uniform with Graded Lessons had already begun. This is not meant as an invidious criticism, but simply as a statement of fact. At any rate progress in religious educational methods has been so rapid and "modern" methods have so quickly become antiquated that most of us are not quite sure whether our schools are modern or not. Of course our principal concern is not that our schools be modern, but that they be efficient. But if we are unprejudiced we realize that new methods generally improve old ones, and that on the whole the new is liable also to be the better method.

What makes Sunday school modern? There was a time when well-oiled mechanical organization was the hallmark of modernity. The earliest schools were often so chaotic that the first cry was for organization. Look over the Sunday school literature of the beginning of this century. It teems with advice on school organization, on the duties of superintendents and secretaries, and plans for Sunday school management. Good organization is as necessary now as it was then but the emphasis has changed from the mechanical to the cultural. The question now is not how smoothly but to what purpose does your Sunday school machine run. The efficiency test has been made much more stringent. Smoothness in organization is still believed to be necessary but the real problem has become how organization may help in developing spiritually cultured young men and young women. One might say that a school is no longer judged by the beauty and power of its machine but by the beauty and strength of its product.

In the second place, emphasis has changed from extensive to intensive development of the Sunday school. In the early stages of Sunday school progress the great ambition was to secure more scholars. This was a worthy ambition because the school could not begin to teach children until it had them. Millions of children were without religious education. To get these children many methods, devices and schemes were invented. Many of these devices were efficient and fruitful. They have not become antiquated and ought still be used. We never have as many children in our school as we might have and we ought to continue to get more. But it is only fair to say that a school is no longer modern simply because it knows how to work all the devices which advertise a school and increase its attendance. Intensive development, by which is meant educational efficiency, has come not to supplant but to supplement extensive activities. We are still trying by more means than one to get more people into our schools but we realize that the principal means is to make the school educationally efficient. We are more intent upon making lessons interesting so that the pupil will want to come, and upon making them profitable, so that it will be worth while for him to come. Everywhere old standards are being re-examined to determine whether they have the highest possible educational efficiency. Teachers are trained so that they may be proficient in their work, lessons are graded so that they may fit the various needs of different ages and material is chosen to make the most effective appeal possible to the scholar. The Sunday school leaders of our own church can not receive too much credit for insisting upon this intensive development in the heat of a great Increase Campaign. We still need campaigns and "drives" and devices and schemes to increase our attendance. But we are not modern simply because we have them. We must realize that even the outward growth of the school is largely dependent upon its intensive development of its educational efficiency.

In the third place, there has been a change of emphasis from subject matter to the object of teaching. Not the text book but the child is our principal concern. The Bible will never be displaced as our text book but we no longer believe that there is a magic efficacy in learning its texts. We are teaching the Bible because we recognize it as a guide of spiritual life, and spiritual life is what we want to develop. It will not be amiss to say that the modern religious educator is choosing biblical material with greater care than he used to, and also that he will ultimately not be able to escape the use of some extra-Biblical material. The emphasis on the child has made the grading of lesson material so urgent and it will not be long before we will all have to admit that we are not modern, and aboveall not efficient, if we do not grade our lessons according to the mental and spiritual capacity of our children. Few of our Evangelical schools are graded (the writer's school is not), graded in the modern meaning of that term. Possibly it is well not to be too precipitate in introducing Graded Lessons. We must first make sure that we as teachers are able to use the Graded Lessons effectively. It will take much thought and preparation to modernize our schools in this phase of the work. We may have to wait upon better preparation for this work but we cannot wait with the preparation. The development of grading is inevitable, and tho we must be cautious we dare not procrastinate.

Even while the emphasis changed from text to child, progress continued and included not only the child but the man. The Bible school is still in a sense the church of the child but it has also become the school of the church. It is the teaching agency of the church. We must reach every one in and thru our schools. Our schools are no longer "Kinderlehre."

These are some phases of modern Sunday school progress. That progress has been swift but also sane. We ought to be sure whether we have kept abreast of that progress not because we believe in modernity for its own sake, but because we want to be as wise as the children of the world and work in His vineyard by the latest methods because they are generally the best.

[The title of this piece which appeared in *The Evangelical Teacher* in July, 1918 in no way alerts readers to its content. Yet here Niebuhr addressed the two key issues within his denomination during the First World War, patriotism and the language question. It was written in his official capacity as Executive Secretary of the War Welfare Commission.]

10. The Present Day Task of the Sunday School

There are so many phases of present problems and tasks that may properly be termed "patriotic," a discussion of which would be appropriate in a patrotic number of the "Teacher" that I hardly know upon which to place most emphasis, and which to discuss. I might very well devote a whole article to the details of a Sunday school's patriotic program of work and emphasize that there should be flags, service flags, and honor rolls in every school and church, that these insignia should be displayed, not only in the whole school, but in the individual classes who have members in national service; that the boys should be presented with Testaments and other good literature upon their departure; that each school should keep in close touch with its enlisted men by means of a varied program of correspondence which should include letters from delegated individuals, letters signed by the whole class, picture and puzzle letters; that kits and other tokens of interest should be sent from time to time; that the letters of the men should be read in the Sunday sessions; that the school should serve not only the men but the nation by placing its organization and enthusiasm at the disposal of community campaigns for the various war charities, and that the Sunday school help the church support its men with the War Welfare Commission so that the services of the whole Evangelical Church will be made available for the men of your Church.

But all of these details of service have been emphasized again

THE PRESENT DAY TASK OF THE SUNDAY SCHOOL

and again, and if any Sunday school is not engaged in definite service the War Welfare Commission will be glad to send it its own literature and that of the General War Time Commission of the Churches which is full of suggestions for every kind of service which may be rendered by every organization in the church during war time.

Just at present my interest is frankly not in this detailed program but in the larger problems of loyalty and patriotism. It is perfectly possible to display flags and sing patriotic airs and pray for our soldiers, and yet not be wholeheartedly with our country. It is even possible to support the Liberty Loans and the Red Cross liberally without having our heart in the right place. The social pressure which is brought to bear upon each individual in these various campaigns is so great that the motives in giving may often be justly suspected of being mixed. Paul correctly distinguishes between real love and its seeming outward manifestation when he says, "Tho I bestow all my goods to feed the poor, and have not love it profiteth me nothing." It is actually possible to support a nation financially and yet not love it. We can not therefore present our contributions in various campaigns as prima facie evidence of our loyalty.

We are not really loyal to this nation until and unless we are loyal to its ideals and principles. There has been in some circles very little understanding of and appreciation for those ideals of democracy which have always guided America.

There has been a too ready admiration of the "efficiency" of monarchies. Monarchies are without a doubt efficient but they pay a price for that efficiency, and they pay it in human liberty. Our fathers decided that they would have liberty first and as much efficiency as would be compatible with that liberty. Incidentally the war is teaching us that a little more efficiency may be compatible with liberty than we had traditionally supposed. But that is neither here nor there. The point is that we do not really love America until we love it, not only because we happened to be born here, but because we understand its principles and believe in its ideals. We ought to love America, not only as one loves a blood relative, but as one loves a friend. It may seem peculiar to place friendship above blood relationship, but if it is based upon a kinship of ideals and principles it does actually stand higher. We remember how Christ said to His followers who announced the coming of His mother and brothers: "Who is My mother? and who are My brethren? Behold My mother and My brethren. For whosoever shall do the will of My Father which is in heaven the same is My brother, and sister, and mother." It is possible for blood relatives to love each other not only because they are related in the flesh, but because a spiritual kinship exists between them. But if this is not the case the love of friends with whom we are working for common ideals stands higher. The patriotism of the nations of the old world is more or less race patriotism. It is based upon blood relationship with the race. But American patriotism is not based on relationship with a race but in loyalty to the institutions and ideals of democracy. An American race has hardly developed, and we can therefore not claim to be related to it. If we are at one with America at all we must be at one with her in her ideals and conceptions of political freedom.

But patriotism is being measured today by even more definite standards than those we have considered. It is regrettable that so many avowals of patriotism content themselves with a declaration of loyalty to the traditional principles of America and an expression of willingness to support the nation, without making reference to the great struggle in which we are engaged. The test of loyalty at the present time is a very specific one. It is: Do you believe in the justice of the American cause in this great conflict? Answering that question for myself, and, I believe, for most Americans of German descent, I am willing to answer the question without equivocation. I do not believe that any nation ever tried more diligently and honorably to avoid a conflict than our nation did, and, being forced finally to enter, that any nation has ever placed the issues of a conflict upon a higher moral plane than ours. American entrance into the war has given the conflict a new meaning. What began as a crime is ending as a crusade and for the first time in the history of the world we have the inspiring spectacle of a nation making every sacrifice of blood and treasure for aims which do not include territorial ambitions or plans for imperial aggrandizement. Except to the hopelessly prejudiced the word of the President that "we wish nothing for ourselves except what we may share with all free peoples," is convincing.

Those of us who are born in America of German descent are not insensible of the fact that this war is being waged against the nation which once claimed the allegiance of our fathers, and to which they are still bound by a thousand sentimental ties. Neither are we indifferent to the soul agonies which such a conflict inflicts upon them. We believe that the nation may well be lenient toward them if they do not find it in their hearts to support the present war as vigorously as we of the second generation do, provided, of course, that there is no transgression of wartime law. In Europe the process of transferring allegiance is not completed in centuries and we ought therefore not be impatient if it is not completed in one generation here. But it ought to be completed in the second generation and it generally is. The writer believes himself to be acquainted with about as many soldiers of German descent as any man. His files are full of letters from them, and they all bear witness to the undivided allegiance of the sons of German parents to the nation of their birth.

Some of the facts mentioned may have no particular relation to Sunday school problems and I have dwelt upon them merely because I knew that in the "Teacher" I had an audience of American-born Americans to whom these problems are vital at the present time. There is another phase of our problem, however, that is particularly vital to Sunday school workers. I refer to the language question. It is obviously possible to be patriotic without knowing the language of a country, but it is just as obviously more difficult. Any nation would be foolish to forgo the advantage of knowing the language of other peoples, because it makes their thoughts and achievements available to it. It would be foolish on the part of America to attempt the complete extermination of the German language in view of the fact that so many achievements in science, art and thought have had that language as their vehicle. But is it not equally senseless to make even a half-hearted attempt to maintain the German language as a means of common intercourse? Let us not delude ourselves. That is just what many of us have been trying to do. We claimed to be maintaining the language for the sake of its cultural value while as a matter of fact we were attempting to establish and maintain it as a common social currency. If we use the German language in Sunday schools this is more clearly established than if we use it in church service. In the church service the use of the German language is in most cases simply a matter of offering the people what they best understand, but when we use the German language in our schools we are forcing it upon American-born Americans and in doing it we are neither American nor completely Christian. We have long since realized that we sacrifice a great deal of pedagogical effectiveness if we teach religion in a language in which the children do not think. If we do it in spite of that fact, we simply confess that we are more interested in the maintenance of a language than in the propagation of religious life.

THE PRESENT DAY TASK OF THE SUNDAY SCHOOL

Nor is the attempt to keep the German language alive as a means of common social intercourse completely American. A nation that accepts immigrants from every corner of the world so freely, as does America, certainly has the right to expect that these immigrants do not attempt to maintain themselves as separate social entities with a language and culture of their own. If they would all do that, America could not be a united nation but would be nothing more than a polyglot rabble of peoples. It is unconvincing to call attention to the various languages which are maintained in other nations, because in practically every one of these nations the use of more than one language is a devisive factor in the nation's life. Austria speaks many languages and for that reason Austria is a poorly united nation that is only held together by a dynasty and not by a community spirit. Canada permitted Quebec to make French rather than English the basic language, with the result that Quebec is constantly at loggerheads with the Dominion. On the other hand there is a good reason for permitting another language when the people have been subjugated, even at the risk of imperiling complete unity. But the millions of immigrants who have come to the shores of America were not subjugated by force, but came here of their own free will, and it is their duty to enter as completely as possible into the whole national life of the country. Heretofore the nation has not Americanized them by force, and we feel confident that it will not do so in the future. The immigrant must pay his debt for this toleration by not forcibly hindering the natural processes of Americanization in his children.

In view of these facts and in view of the special emphasis given them by the tragic events of the hour every Sunday school that is still bilingual, ought very seriously consider the abolition of the German in the Sunday schools. Irrespective of every other consideration the somewhat prevalent habit of teaching our classes with the explanations in English but with the use of German lessons helps in a crime against good taste and common sense, and ought to be stopped.

[As Executive Secretary of the War Welfare Commission Niebuhr was frequently engaged in speaking and writing about his Church's position in relation to the war. This article contributed to *The Keryx* in October, 1918 provides an excellent summary of his own standpoint and is especially useful when looking at his more mature Second World War view of Christian participation.]

II. A Message From Reinhold Niebuhr

I have been asked by the editor of the Keryx to contribute an article on some subject related to the great world war and America's participation in it. I know of no subject falling in this category that would be of greater interest than an analysis of pacifism in its relation to patriotism. Most ministers were or are pacifists. It is to their credit that they were. The church has no business breeding war spirit or readily sanctioning war plans.

Some ministers are still pacifists. It might be better to say that all ministers and all Christians ought to be pacifists in the best sense of the term but that some are still so unqualifiedly opposed to war that they refuse to aid the nation in its present wartime and perform such duties as are demanded of them with a noticeable lack of enthusiasm. Are they the only sincere Christians and are the rest of us who support the nation wholeheartedly apostates of the true faith? The problem is one that needs analysis. To set ourselves against the best purposes of a nation and to refuse cooperation in an undertaking which is supported by so much Christian idealism is a rather serious policy of conduct that no one ought to be willing to adopt without much searching of heart.

The crux of the whole question of pacifism is its sincerity. Almost every nation engaged in this war respects conscientious scruples. Of course it is obvious that even sincerity can not always gain immunity for our convictions if those convictions lead to actions and conduct that are harmful to the state. But most nations, particularly democratic nations, are very tolerant of opinion not in conformity with the temper of the people provided it is honest beyond a doubt. This tolerance is naturally somewhat restricted by the passion of war times but it has never been completely abandoned.

The question then is, if we are still pacifists, is our pacifism honest? Every man naturally believes his own opinions to be sincere but that conviction is no guarantee for this honesty. There is a great deal of unconscious insincerity. Unconscious dishonesty or sincere insincerity may seem to be a psychological anomaly but it is not necessarily. Many influences and motives of which we are not conscious determine our actions so that it frequently occurs that we do things with a fine consciousness of virtue while others see ulterior motives in our actions; this probably accounts for the fact that we frequently have a more favorable opinion of ourselves than others have.

The first test to which we might put our pacifism is this: Are we opposed to all war or are we opposed only to this particular war? There seems to be quite a number of men who have developed religious scruples against war very recently. They never protested against the military ambitions of Germany or any other nation. Sometimes they were even inclined to sneer at the "sentimental" hopes of the world for a permanent peace. Perhaps they even proved from the prophets that the world was bound to take its end in the midst of a great war and that therefore all peace hopes were unbiblical. If this has been their position they have no cause for complaint if the world will not accept their opposition to this war as genuine. The only possible cause for opposition to this war is a very genuine opposition to all war because as wars go there has never been one that

A MESSAGE FROM REINHOLD NIEBUHR

had in it so much Christian idealism and that was so full of purpose to use the sacrifices of war for its final abolition.

But there have been many ministers of the gospel, sincere servants of Christ, who once professed themselves as opposed to all war who are now nevertheless supporting the present martial venture and adventure of America. What shall we say of them? Have they permitted themselves to be carried away by passion of the hour and have they sacrificed principles and convictions for the sake of popular favor? Tho we can readily admit that the voice of the pulpit has often been too strident and that it has too easily become the vehicle of vindicative passions, it must be said that many ministers are entirely Christian in their support of the war and perfectly sincere in changing their position on the war. Pacifism has only one chance of becoming a power for peace and that is that it will woo others to its ideals. If an isolated attempt to maintain moral order without the use of force fails to impress the rest of the world it must be abandoned for a time, or at least applied less rigorously, or the idealism which prompted it will be the cause of its own defeat. Too often has righteousness been defeated in history because its champions refused to make compromises on methods in order to bring victory to their principles.

This was the position of America in the great war. No nation was more definitely committed to the peace ideal than ours. We loved peace and we were willing to go to almost any length to maintain it. But when the world, particularly our present enemies, misinterpreted this idealism and sneeringly construed it as a rich and flabby complacency that was afraid to risk the prosperity of peace in the fortunes of war, we began to realize that our very love of peace might cause us to lose it. Our words of admonishment to Europe, even our threats went unheeded because the world looked upon us as being too pacifist to support our threats with action. Thus while we tried to be innocent as doves we also learned to be wise as serpents. Of course there is a danger of becoming too wise and too cynical and not risking enough for our ideals. If we were all "Realpolitiker" and if we reckoned only with the passions and the sins of men as they actually exist and if we had not faith at all in the ability of men to meet the challenge of ideals the world would never progress. We must venture beyond the accepted standards of the world or there will be no progress, but we must not venture farther than the world can follow us or our progress will collapse.

To some this policy of compromising for the sake of righteousness may seem dubious. They will say that the heroes of righteousness whose memories we honor did not follow this course. They were uncompromising protagonists of their ideals. Even if we admit that they were—an admission which would be obviously gratuitous in some cases, in that of Martin Luther for instance—it would yet remain a fact that the prophets of righteousness who made no compromises could not have achieved their ideals but for the statesman who did make compromises. Abraham Lincoln was just as necessary to the abolition movement as William Lloyd Garrison. Christian statesmen are essential to the kingdom of God as Christian prophets. But, you will say, it is the business of the church to perform the prophet's and not the statesman's task, and for that reason it is justified in an uncompromising opposition to war. For that very reason let us honor those who assume the prophetic function and who by their uncompromising adherence to an ideal keep the goal for which we are striving before us, and prevent us from compromising too much. We may well lament the fact that so many of the best prophets of peace are not in the pulpit, not even in the church, Bertrand Russell for example.

Prophets are necessarily in the minority however, and their ethics must be "minority ethics." The Christian church has either by choice or by the logic of history become the religious institution, not of an eclectic minority, but of nations. It must therefore speak to the nations and must be statesmanlike as well as prophetic. If it is best for nations not to hold to the ideal of peace without compromise the church, insofar as it is responsible for national action, is only doing its duty when it counsels in favor of the compromise that is necessary for the achievement of the ideal. Even the Quakers are secure in their pacifism only because they are a sect. They would have to deny their pacifism were they responsible for national action, and national policies. Their security lies in their irresponsibility.

When once this compromise has been made it ought to be the chief duty of those who are interested in ideals to be vigilant that the ideals be not lost in the struggle. The church ought to regard this vigilance over the moral aims of the war as its principal task. It will gain more by influencing the ideals of the war than by withholding its support altogether. We can be thankful as American Christians that our aims have real moral value inasmuch as they are not selfish or national but are concerned with a new international order and organization. As between our enemies and our allies there seems to be rather more moral purpose to end war for all time with our allies; as between our allies and ourselves our own aims seem to be freer of imperialistic and nationalistic motives than theirs; among ourselves the president defines our aims more idealistically and lays more stress upon international aims than press or pulpit or public opinion. We can see, therefore, that while we have aims in this war, which may well justify a Christian to support it, a Christian ought not support war without constant insistence that the aims be moral and that the ends for which war is being waged shall contribute to its final abolition.

There are enemies of peace within our own borders and among our friends. War necessarily enlists all sorts and conditions of people and there are some in the ranks of democracy and some even at its counsel tables who do not want a new international order which will make further imperial expansion impossible. The best thing that pacifists can do is fight these enemies of a lasting peace. It is a regrettable fact that the democratic liberalism and international idealism of President Wilson has received more support from the ranks of political liberals than from organized Christianity. The church has done little to marshal the force of public opinion behind the president's peace program. In England the British Labor Party and not the English church has made itself the protagonist of the president's program. In America the president seems to meet with even less understanding than among British liberals. Here is a real opportunity for liberal spirits in the church who are opposed to war.

I have just read again the president's fourth liberty loan speech in which he declares that there can be neither economic boycotts nor special international ententes in a league of nations and in which he further defines the constitution of such a league. No one who has read the president's state utterances with an unbiased mind can fail to see that he is continually raising the aims for which the nations are striving. The very hope of the world and of civilization seems to lie in these aims. If the president succeeds in making them dominant and if the final peace conference will not content itself with territorial readjustments but will dedicate its energies to the abolition of international anarchy and the establishment of international order, civilization will be saved. If not, the war will have been lost no matter who wins it. This is the issue and the course for pacifists ought to be plain. Those who love peace must fashion the forces of war in the interest of their ideal and not content themselves with futile opposition to the war itself.

[As Niebuhr explained in a letter to Synod President Baltzer, "Where Shall We Go?" (published in the March, 1919 issue of the *Magazin für Evangelische Theologie und Kirche*, the Synod's theological journal) grew out of his participating in the "Conference on Organic Union of the Church," which had been called by the General Assembly of the Presbyterian Church in the U.S.A. for the purpose of formulating a plan of organic union. One hundred representatives of 17 denominations took part in the meeting which was held December 4-6, 1918 in Philadelphia. This article was written for inclusion in the denominational newspaper, *The Evangelical Herald*, but Baltzer found it good enough to insist it be in the *Magazin* where it could better stimulate debate.]

12. Where Shall We Go?

In the closing months of 1918 two conferences were held which may mean much in the religious history of America and which beyond their historical interest have special significance for our own Evangelical church. The one was the merger conference of the United Lutheran Church in America in which three of the more liberal Lutheran synods were united into one formidable Lutheran church, which promises to absorb other Lutheran bodies and, with the possible exception of the Missouri stronghold, to present a united Lutheranism in America.

The other conference was the one in Philadelphia called upon invitation of the Presbyterian General Assembly to consider the prospects and means of uniting American protestantism into an "organic union." The very fact that this conference was held marks what may become an epoch making step in religious history of America. But the conference resulted in specific developments which are of even greater importance. Among these may be mentioned the new attempt to unite all Calvinistic churches in America even before a general union is undertaken. Every one who attended the conference must have been impressed with the great obstacles which still lie in the way of a complete union of American protestantism even tho the fact that these obstacles appear less insurmountable than they once did is equally impressive. The conference may or may not be the beginning of a movement which will result in the organic union of protestantism in America in the not too distant future; but one can not escape the conviction that, whatever may be its significance for a general union of protestantism, it did undoubtedly encourage and hasten "family reunions" among American denominations. Among such possible family reunions a Calvinistic one is most immediately probable.

In other words the situation is that we may soon have a united Lutherdom and a united Calvinism with the possibility of further unions which will eliminate practically all so-called minor denominations and leave only several large and distinctive churches. This situation is one of tremendous significance for us, both because we are a small church and because we are a denomination that is historically related to both Lutheran and Calvinistic bodies. What attitude shall we assume toward these new developments and what policy must we formulate?

One possible policy is to have no policy at all or to abide in our present attitude without recognizing that "New occasions teach new duties." We can claim that our development of protestant religious culture is so very distinctive that we can not possibly sacrifice any part of its uniqueness by merging it with others. That is a position quite generally held. There are many of us who regard it as untenable. It verges on an egotism that is as ridiculous as it is sublime. It may be sublime in the sense that it can be supported only by a great faith but it is ridiculous in that it lacks a sense of proportion. It does not take into account that we are not only a very small denomination but also that we have failed to make any very distinctive contribution to

WHERE SHALL WE GO?

American religious life. We have served our Lord faithfully and have labored in the part of the Kingdom entrusted to us but we certainly can not claim to have left the impress of our personality upon the religious thought of our country. In a large city it is a common sight to find whole blocks of flats so alike that they can not be distinguished from each other. Any one of these flats does not contribute anything to the architectural beauty of the city but if you were permitted into the privacy of one of them you would find a most distinctive atmosphere there that is created by the family that lives in it, by its habits and traditions and customs. The distinction of our religious culture is like the inside of the flat and our lack of uniqueness is like the outside of it. You find it very difficult to get some families to abandon their flat for one very much like it because their association with it has invested it with a charm that they appreciate even tho the world can not sense it. So we would find it very difficult to abandon our particular house in the kingdom of God if we were asked to move into larger quarters. We appreciate the atmosphere of our home and the sanctity which tradition gives it even if these subtle things escape the larger world. Such an attitude may be excusably natural and human but it may be as unchristian as it is human.

Another possible policy toward the union developments is to assert our sympathy for them but to claim that inasmuch as we are a union church, the ultimate union must be built upon our foundation. The presumption of this position is even greater than that of the first. There are other churches much larger than our own that have similar traditions of church union in their denominational thought world (the Disciples and Episcopalians for instance), and they have not only been more ambitious to assert their positions, but were in a better position to do so. Their ambition has availed them little, and ours will avail us even less, because the churches are not very tolerant of cut and dried methods of church union which generally turn out to be nothing more than attempts to absorb other churches with a maximum sacrifice of denominational position on their part and a minimum sacrifice on yours.

There are several other facts that make our unionistic position untenable: 1) It takes into consideration only the Lutheran and Reformed churches and has no appreciation for the distinctive personalities of other church bodies grown strong on American soil. One of our theologians has in fact taught that the division between the Lutheran and Reformed church is the only legitimate division of protestantism, other denominations being no more than sects. 2) Inasfar as it takes the Lutheran church into consideration it is futile for the Lutheran church has never shown the slightest inclination toward union with any other denomination. The present ambition of the Lutheran church is a united Lutheranism and not a united Protestantism. 3) We have not accomplished a real union between Calvinism and Lutheranism in our own church. Our church is far more Lutheran than Reformed in polity and tradition.

The first step, than, toward the adoption of an adequate policy for the modern situation is the acquisition of a finer Christian modesty and a greater readiness to accommrodate ourselves to the positions of other denominations than those with which our tradition is connected.

But since we are still far from a general reunion of all American protestantism this does not solve our problem. What shall we do if in the near future we are confronted by a united Calvinism and a united Lutheranism? We can not unite the two any more than Canada will be able to be the instrument of a rapprochement between, let us say, British and American world politics. If we can not be the instrument of union here (and even our strongest apostles of union have lacked the

WHERE SHALL WE GO?

ambition to make any practical attempt in this direction) we can not be the instrument of union anywhere. Our only alternatives of policy are then, to remain a small denomination in a day in which small denominations are disappearing or to join forces with one of these two protestant denominations with which we are most closely allied by tradition, theology and custom.

Shall we join the new Lutheran coalition? Many voices have been heard in our church favoring such a step. But we can hardly go where we are not wanted and there is nothing clearer than that we are not wanted in the new coalition except upon a strictly Lutheran basis. For it must be emphasized, tho this fact does not yet seem to be generally known among us, that the new Lutheran union is laid upon the most orthodox foundation. Whatever liberalism the General Synod had was sacrificed in favor of the union. In fact to an outsider the union seems in many respects not so much a union as an absorption by the General Council of two other Lutheran bodies, both more liberal than itself. The credal foundation of the union is the U. L. C. and the accent seems to be upon the U. The ambition of the new church seems to be to absorb in time some of the even more orthodox Lutheran bodies and to present a united Lutheranism in America. In such a scheme we would have no place except by sacrificing everything that has distinguished our Evangelical position. There may be some marks of alleged distinction which we ought to be willing to sacrifice in favor of a united protestantism but it would certainly be illogical on our part to sacrifice our principles of union for the sake of a union, which in the ultimate sense, does not unite but divide. Tho in a general way we have always been more Lutheran than Reformed, it is obvious then, that a further rapprochement with Lutheranism is impossible.

The final alternative may now be adduced from our rejection of the first. Shall we fly into the arms of Calvinism? Many will say, that is just as impossible as the first alternative proposed. We are not Calvinistic. But to this we might reply, neither is Calvinism. So-called Calvinism is certainly less Calvinistic than Lutheranism is Lutheran. One of the speakers at the Philadelphia conference pointedly observed that Calvinism had always been irenic ever since Zwingli offered Luther his hand in pledge of brotherly love, tho he did not say that Lutheranism had been separatistic ever since Luther refused to take Zwingli's hand. In fact the proposed union of Calvinistic churches is a union of presbyterianism more than a union of Calvinism.

Theological obstacles to such a union would be practically nil. The ancient (and may we not say antedated?) difference between the Reformed and the Lutheran church on the Lord's Supper need not bother us. Our position is that this difference is non-essential and in a less explicit way that is the position of Calvinism. It is the Lutheran church which declares the difference essential. And even beyond our official position in this matter it can not be denied that the view which our laymen and also our younger clergy hold in regard to the Lord's Supper approaches the position of Zwingli more nearly than that of Luther, even tho we were sometimes taught in our seminaries that Luther's doctrine of the Supper was "more profound." Some of us will not be afraid to say that Luther's theology of the Lord's Supper was not so much a distinctive theological position as it was an attempt to compromise with catholicism, and its *opus operatum* view of the sacraments.

There are some who think that Calvinism has an entirely different religious philosophy underlying it than that of the Lutheran world-view to which we have adhered. They say that the Lutheran position emphasizes the grace of God in the plan of salvation while Calvinism is moralistic and makes salvation too much a matter of our own enterprise. It is true, that Calvinism is traditionally moralistic while Lutheranism is traditionally

WHERE SHALL WE GO?

quietistic. Calvin was ambitious to influence political life in Geneva and John Knox was a prophet in Scotland while Luther religiously refrained, as far as he could, from exerting influence upon social-political problems in Germany. Calvinism has been moralistic in the best sense of the word. If there has been an overemphasis in American church life upon the need of personal effort in finding salvation that has been Methodistic and not Calvinistic. If Luther emphasized the grace of God, Calvin dwelt upon His omnipotence just as insistently. Surely a theology that has the tradition of predestination in it can not be accused of being too moralistic.

Our difficulties in uniting with Calvinism will be difficulties of polity rather than difficulties of theology. Our polity, our church forms and customs are prevailingly Lutheran, but they are not so prevailingly Lutheran as they once were. Our younger and more English churches and our younger ministers have often departed from our ancient customs much to the discomfort of their older brothers. Yet in the majority of our churches difficulty would be found in this respect. But matters of polity have been the curse of the Christian church. What does the Lord care, whether we wear pulpit gowns (tho no one would ask us to discard them) or whether we receive communion at the altar or in our pews, or what the liturgical order of our service may be. If these differences seem important to us, tho we must admit that laymen as well as ministers have held them important, we are only revealing one of the worst weaknesses of the religious-minded against which Jesus and the prophets contended.

In a possible union with Calvinistic churches some would fear to lose our cherished rite of confirmation, tho many Calvinistic churches have preserved the rite. But even where the rite in our distinctive form has not been preserved, there is a more and more general recognition of the fact that children of church members should be received into the church after a normal religious development that must be guided by education and that is the fundamental thought in our confirmation with which we will not part. As far as some of the distinctive features of our confirmation go we ought to be ready and willing to part with them. Our confirmation does not sufficiently encourage a spontaneous decision for Christ on the part of the child. Many ministers are able to make confirmation something that is a little more spontaneous but the tradition is against it and the unchurched hangers-on of our churches still persist in forcing their children or at least in ordering them to be confirmed simply because that was the way of their fathers. And any one versed in modern developments of pedagogy must admit that our catechism is a pedagogical monstrosity. Children are asked to learn meaningless definitions and, except if constant influence is exerted to the contrary, to look upon confirmation instruction as gymnastics in the art of learning by wrote.

Perhaps actual difficulties can not be overcome as easily in fact as upon paper, but there are sufficient reasons why we should at least seriously consider the denominational policy here indicated.

[Reaction to "Where Shall We Go?" came swiftly. In the following issue of the *Magazin für Evangelische Theologie und Kirche* a reply, "Why Go At All?" appeared written by an influential pastor, W.F. Henninger. In the July, 1919 number Niebuhr responded.]

13. In Rebuttal, by the Author of "Where Shall We Go?"

With a good deal of interest I have read the answer to my question "Where Shall We Go?" in the form of a counter question "Why Go at All?" in the May issue of your magazine. I have no wish to prolong the argument indefinitely but I think you owe me a few words in the columns of your journal to call the attention of your readers to some very specious reasoning on the part of my opponent.

An attempt is made to refute my statement that we are a small denomination by pointing to the fact that we are 15th in a list of 165 denominations. The writer fails to say however that there are fifteen times as many communicants in the 14 denominations that are larger than we than in the 150 that are smaller. You can do anything with statistics. We are a small denomination. We need no statistical evidence for that. Every one of us actually engaged in the work of our church meets constant proof of our numerical weakness. If any more proof is needed than that which every one has at hand we might point to the fact that we do not even consider ourselves large enough to maintain adequate educational facilities for our young men and women. We are going to get a junior college now but my disillusioned and discouraged opinion is that it will be twenty years before we have a real A. B. college.

A similar attempt is made to refute my assertion that small

denominations are disappearing. Again statistics are dragged in and evidence presented that in the past ten years small denominations have not decreased. That is all beside the point. The whole point of my argument rested upon the fact that in the past few months union movements, particularly family reunion movements have been launched that bid fair to eliminate small denominations. What happened in the past ten years has nothing to do with the facts which we are facing now.

The writer of the article under consideration did me the favor of proving my contention that most of the pastors of our church regard only the Lutheran-Calvinistic division of protestantism as legitimate, by going to great lengths to establish that all protestant denominations have an element of either Lutheran or Calvinistic theology. What of that? A baptist might just as well point out that all churches are either immersionists or sprinklers and conclude from that that the question of the mode of baptism is the one fundamental one in protestantism. To what impossible conclusions such reasoning leads may be seen by the fact that it betrays the writer to describe Methodism as Calvinistic. Methodism, as everyone ought to know is Arminian and not Calvinistic and the question of free will which divides Arminianism and Calvinism may be regarded as just as fundamental as the differences of opinion between Lutheran and Calvinistic theology. Precisely because we fail to have any sympathy for these other differences we are not fitted to play the role of mediator between many of the American denominations.

My final remarks in regard to confirmation were so completely misunderstood by Brother Henninger that one is persuaded that he did not try very hard to get their meaning. If there is anything in our Evangelical polity that I believe in it is confirmation, and I made the statement that we could never afford to part with the fundamental idea of confirmation which is that a Christian child need *not be converted* but should grow gradually

IN REBUTTAL, BY THE AUTHOR OF "WHERE SHALL WE GO?"

into Christian convictions and decisions. I did assert however that confirmation should encourage spontaneous decisions for Christ and that the traditional way of conducting confirmation classes and confirmation rites did not provide for or encourage this element of spontaneity. From what Brother Henninger says about conversion one would judge that he does not believe in conversions at all. If he does not I can not help but call his attention to the fact that he is doubting a fundamental Christian and Biblical fact. If there is no such thing as conversion then all our preaching is vain. Just because we may not believe that violent and cataclysmic conversions are normal methods for children to enter the kingdom of God we ought not to permit ourselves to deny a fundamental religious fact. Incidentally it might also be observed that if all conversions do not prove "water tight" neither do all confirmations. Will Brother Henninger tell us whether fifty per cent of all young men and women he has confirmed in the past ten years are active church members? If they are he is more fortunate than most of us. In the past ten years we have confirmed more young men and women than the entire number of our active church members. That does not discredit confirmation in itself but it ought to teach us to be a little modest and refrain from adopting an air of superiority when reviewing religious methods other than our own.[1]

---

[1] Niebuhr's basic proposal continued to be debated for the next decade until it became clear that consultation with the Reformed Church in the United States was the logical direction to take. Indeed, just prior to the establishment of a "Commission on Closer Relations with Other Church Bodies" to develop the foundation for an actual merger, Niebuhr wrote a letter to the Editor of the *Theological Magazine* (the new name of the *Magazin für Evangelische Theologie und Kirche*) in which he restated his position: "The only other group remaining with which we have any common heritage is the *Reformed church*. Its membership is drawn from the same kind of people as our own and its whole temper is very similar to our own . . . A *union* with *the Reformed church* would create a denomination of some six hundred thousand communicants. A denomination of this size could carry on its missionary and educational tasks with much less waste than our respective denominations under present conditions. There would be more than this advantage in union however. A union of

[This address was delivered at the Second National Convention of Evangelical Sunday Schools which took place in Chicago from July 24-29, 1919. In spite of broadening interests Niebuhr was still considered an expert on educational matters and he continued to rally for the improvement of Church Schools.]

14. Educational Principles in Church Schools

The Sunday school has passed through different stages of development. It began as a slum institute for the poor children, and was at that time a secular institution.

In the second period it became recognized as a valuable adjunct to the church. In this period the uniform lessons were introduced and great emphasis was laid upon learning the Bible. The Bible was divided into so many lessons for so many Sundays. These lessons were taken from the Old Testament in proportion to its size without regard for their intrinsic value, with the result that the New Testament was neglected and the Old Testament had more than its share.

The third period began about 1890 and might be called the expansion period. In this period emphasis was placed upon large numbers; in fact, numbers were worshiped. A good Sunday school was one that had numbers. It was also the organization period. A great emphasis was placed upon methods, plans and

---

the two churches would bring fresh life and inspiration to both parties. It would result in a denomination which could make a real contribution to American church life. Perhaps the idea is a wild one. When suggested some years ago by the present writer in the pages of this magazine it was hailed with derision. There is good reason however to believe that the present temper of the church is not so unsympathetic toward the proposal." Thus, Niebuhr played a decisive role in suggesting the pattern that led to the merger of the Evangelical and Reformed Church in 1934 and there is also some evidence to suggest that he worked behind the scenes in those years to help bring it about. For the complete text of Niebuhr's letter to the Editor see "To the Editor," *Theological Magazine of the Evangelical Synod of North America*, Vol. 56, No. 1 (January, 1928), pp. 49-50.

schemes, and the literature of the Sunday school treated mainly the problems of organiziation. Campaigns were considered as great things to bring the children in, but little emphasis was placed upon efficiency in the Sunday school to keep the children in.

We have now reached the period called the educational period. Expansion has ceased to be our chief concern; we are trying to make the Sunday school an educational institution.

The ideals of the modern Sunday schools are educational. Formerly the Sunday school was defined as the church for the child, but now it is becoming the school of the church. This tendency is seen both in church and Sunday school architecture. At first the Sunday school was housed in one room; then it met in nooks and corners, but now we have classrooms for every class.

Not knowledge but culture is the goal — not trying to infiltrate knowledge but to inculcate culture. We once thought that we were all right if we knew all the biblical facts. Now, we have not given up biblical teaching; we need the text-book, and the Bible is still our text book, but we are going to be more careful about choosing the material for the purpose of presenting the truths that we are to teach. We are going to choose the text material with reference to the child, and with the child as the object. Thus we shall place the emphasis upon the culture rather than upon knowledge.

In developing personality we must treat the child with reference to its nature and demands. The smallest child has as big a soul as the biggest man. The little child needs just as finished teaching as the man, since each has its own laws and characteristics. We cannot be satisfied merely with the teaching of facts, but must strive for the development of spiritual personality. Thus we are going to make use of biblical knowledge to bring about spiritual culture.

Modern teaching stands for freedom as against authority. What does this mean? Lead the child rather than command it. It is better to help the child discover the truth than to discover the truth for the child. If we weigh this thought carefully we shall see how far we fall short as good teachers. It is easy to tell a child something, but it requires pedagogical talent to help it discover the truth. It is our business to help the child discover conscience and moral order. There is no virtue so much overestimated as authority; there is none so much emphasized as obedience. But fear has no value. Insist upon authority, and you have lost it, and the teacher who has to insist upon obedience is lost. It is far better to show why a thing is wrong. We must substitute our will for theirs and thus bring out a harmony of desires as a matter of natural growth.

Let us lead the child of today to right thinking; lead the child to think about the moral problems involved in their actions — not deciding for them, but making of them co-workers. With a child trained on fear, you cannot hope to make free moral agents. Of course, if we were all ideal pedagogues we would never have to whip children. Sometimes corporal punishment has to be resorted to, but with the right kind of training punishment should not be necessary. Consult with children, both in school and at home, and by their confidence in your superior knowledge and experience spiritual culture will be easy of achievement. You cannot develop moral order on the basis of fear, for it will exist only as long as you have force to maintain it. Based on authority and obedience a reaction is bound to result. Based on respect and confidence, with freedom as the goal, results are bound to follow.

We are looking forward to new developments in the realm of religious education. The Sunday school is breaking down of its own weight, and we shall have to have something more. What shall we have in place of it? Some demand religious instruction in schools. We do not care, however, whether the Bible is read in schools or not. Such reading is not conducive to spiritual culture. We should have a plan big enough to cover the need, and it should be assumed by ourselves. But, if we admit that the Sunday school is not sufficient, what about our parochial schools? I do not look upon their extinction with much sorrow or regret. We cannot have secular education in charge of the church, and we cannot have religious education in control of the state. The emphasis is upon education. When teaching religion you are not teaching mathematics. We need Christians to teach children.

["The Keryx and Our Educational Institutions," again pointed to the urgent need for still more progress in the development of a full four year college at Elmhurst. It appeared in February, 1920.]

15. The Keryx and Our Educational Institutions

I am informed by the editor of the *Keryx* that our valuable little college periodical is about to celebrate its tenth birthday and would appreciate a word from its former editors. It hardly seems possible that ten years should have passed so rapidly. Until I received this news I still fancied myself among the "recent graduates" of Eden but this birthday anniversary forces me to realize that we belong to the "ancients" before we know it.

The *Keryx* has had a profitable ten years of existence. It has served to maintain the interest of our pastors in the educational institutions and has offered ambitious students a vehicle for literary expression. But the real achievement of the *Keryx* has been its successful advocacy of better educational facilities for the young men of our denomination. It was the *Keryx* that first began the agitation for a real college at Elmhurst. Previous to its birth there was only a very feeble demand for a college with higher academic standards than prevailed in Elmhurst but since its inception to this day the *Keryx* has been a voice demanding progress in our educational program. This demand soon gained momentum in the entire church and resulted in the decision of the last General Conference to raise Elmhurst to the standard of a junior college. While the changes at Elmhurst are too recent to be regarded as the complete realization of this aim we may nevertheless be gratified to know that its realization is immanent.

In spite of the progress that has been made there is as yet no cause for complacency. It has taken ten years to accomplish—

THE KERYX AND OUR EDUCATIONAL INSTITUTIONS

what? The changes at Elmhurst so far mean but the addition of one new professor and no addition to the physical equipment of the school except the now contemplated library building. At this rate it will be fifty years before we have a first class A. B. college. As yet there seems to be no definite realization in our church that we can not have what we need in educational advantages without the expenditures of a large amount of money and a program to secure the funds that are needed. Even a good junior college at Elmhurst will require the investment of at least $250,000.00 and a full college is out of the question with less than $500,000.00. Such large sums will never be secured until the interest in our educational institutions is increased to a much greater extent and our needs felt much more keenly and widely than at present.

Probably there are many who admit the need but will not grant the possibility of meeting it if any such sums as have been mentioned are required. Some facts about other denominations and their colleges may dispel these doubts. The United Brethren report almost the same membership as our synod. They have five A. B. colleges and we have none. The new Norwegian amalgamation of synods have 50,000 less communicants than we but have 8 colleges.

The Missouri Synod is roughly three times as large as we are and has 14 colleges, not all of the highest academic standing but nevertheless far ahead of us. The new United Lutheran church is perhaps four times as large as we but has 13 colleges and ten seminaries. The membership of the "Society of Friends" or "Quakers" is about one third of ours and they have 9 colleges, some of them of the very highest standing. The Congregational church has a membership no greater than four times that of our church and there are 40 Congregational colleges in the country. Even the fact that this is a wealthy denomination and one of the oldest in America will not adequately explain the disparity between their educational institutions and ours.

If it were necessary examples could be multiplied. It will suffice to say there is hardly a denomination in America that does not outrank us in educational institutions. Even the negro denominations have not only more colleges for their membership than we but they have several institutions of high scholastic standing and offering degrees recognized by the Carnegie foundation, while we have none.

We have been too long indifferent to our colleges and seminary and have fallen too far behind the procession to make a policy of very gradual development at all acceptable now. We need a heroic attempt to get abreast of other denominations. I hope that the *Keryx* will continue to champion educational progress and that our church will be challenged to undertake something really big in the near future for our educational institutions.

Gustav Niebuhr

Edward J. Hosto

The Niebuhr family on the porch of the parsonage in Lincoln, Illinois. From left to right: Hulda, Walter, H. Richard, Reinhold and Lydia Niebuhr.

The 1909 Elmhurst baseball team. Reinhold Niebuhr is squatting on the left. Paul Zwilling is on the right. The player standing second from right is Carl Schneider.

Reinhold (on left) and Richard Niebuhr (third from right) pose with some classmates at Eden Seminary.

Reinhold Niebuhr as an Eden graduate in 1913.

Bethel Evangelical Church as it looked in 1915.

Reinhold Niebuhr in 1918.

["Shall a Minister Have an Education?" published in the May, 1921 issue of the *Magazin für Evangelische Theologie und Kirche*, was Niebuhr's boldest effort to quiet those opposed to modernizing the denomination's educational institutions. Yet in the months following its publication his stand brought repeated attacks in successive issues of the *Magazin*.]

16. Shall a Minister Have an Education?

The cause of higher education seems well nigh hopeless in our denomination. Four years ago it was decided that we would have a junior college. Efforts have been made in that direction, but our goal has not yet been reached. Elmhurst is not yet a first rate junior college. We have been making progress slowly; but evidently our progress has been too swift for some of the brethren. Not long since one of the Elmhurst professors distributed among all pastors of the church a pamphlet containing an address of which he had unburdened himself at a district conference and which had been evidently received with such marks of approval as to warrant its publication.[1] The burden of the address was that we ought not to give our ministers a college education. If college is absolutely wanted we ought to confer its doubtful benefits upon future doctors and lawyers while we jealously guard our future ministers from the baneful influences of modern science by immersing them in the classical antiquities of Rome and Greece. In the March number of the Theological Magazine another voice of authority is added to support this attitude, curiously enough coming from another

---

[1]The address was by Professor Karl Bauer and was published under the title, *Die Zukunft des Proseminars*. St. Louis: Eden Publishing House, n.d. Bauer was Professor of Greek and Latin at Elmhurst.

professor.[2] Our cause does seem hopeless when our academic leaders, from whom we ought to expect the most enthusiastic support for the cause of higher education, are the very ones who discourage it.

We need not concern ourselves with the charge that Elmhurst is growing too English under the Junior college regime. The language question is being decided by the relentless forces of time, and if anyone wishes to exercise his voice by crying "Back Tides," we can not gainsay him.[3]

What is discouraging is that both professors think that a high school education (for old Elmhurst was little better than a high school) will fit men for the ministry better than a college education. In the one case the physical sciences are ridiculed by pointing out that the dissection of a frog (biological laboratory work) works no benefit upon the mind of a future minister. In the other case not only the physical sciences, but the social sciences and even psychology and philosophy are either ridiculed or damned with faint praise. The answer to this obscurantism is a simple one. Biology is not particularly needed by the minister, but its knowledge is something that belongs to the equipment of every educated man.

We are living in an age of science. Nothing is so outstanding in modern civilization as the tremendous progress which all sciences and particularly the physical sciences have made. They have reshaped all of modern thought, and their achievements

---

[2]Prof. F. Mayer, "Bedenken in Beziehung auf das Proseminar," *Magazin für Evangelische Theologie und Kirche*, Vol. 49, No. 2 (März 1921), pp. 88-91. Mayer was Professor of Practical Theology at Eden Seminary.

[3]One of the major continuing controversies in the Synod was the so-called "language question." The widespread use of English, occasioned by decreased German immigration and the increase of native-born church members, accelerated by the First World War, left some of the older pastors concerned that the especially German character of the Synod would be lost. Both Bauer and Mayer reflect this.

enter consciously and unconsciously into the whole woof and warp of our thinking. If our colleges have made any mistake more glaring than another, it has been to send us into a world which takes evolution for granted, knowing nothing about it except that we have gathered from a few professorial class room jests. Hundreds of our young people are graduating from the colleges of the country having absorbed the scientific viewpoint of the world and with their faith imperiled. The study of science with its necessarily impersonal attitude is bound to imperil those spiritual values which religion conserves, and these values can be saved only if we are wise enough to reinterpret spiritual affirmations in the light of scientific discovery. No one can do this who is blissfully ignorant of the indisputable achievements of science. Many young people are being lost to the church for this very lack.

Even were this not true and if we were willing to rigorously exclude the study of modern science from our colleges for fear that it might imperil the too tender faith of our budding clergymen the need of a college would still be pressing. For a college teaches other things beside science. One of the professors thinks that the study of psychology and sociology is wanted chiefly to give the future minister a little more prestige in his club and civic relationships, and he is afraid that the study of philosophy will dampen the moral ardor so necessary to the prophet. And this same professor waxes eloquent in the defense of a classical against a scientific education! Is not the study of philosophy one of the prime requisites in a classical education? Or does a classical education consists only in the study of Greek and Latin, as the learned professor of Greek and Latin seems to think? It is a rather sorry commentary on the state of our culture that a professor should seriously advance the theory that everything but the study of languages, and perhaps a little history, should be detrimental to future ministers.

YOUNG REINHOLD NIEBUHR: HIS EARLY WRITINGS, 1911-1931

We are living in a world of great complexity. Its social and economic relationships are complex, and if the spirit of the gospel is going to exert any influence upon those relationships it will have to be interpreted by men who do not only understand the gospel but who understand the civilization which they are trying to influence. We are living in a world that has absorbed scientific facts so quickly as to leave many perplexities in regard to the destiny of man and the worth of human personality. To such a world the comfort of the great affirmations of faith can be presented only if we understand what the world is perplexed about. There are altogether too many ministers who are so busy asserting that the gospel is a panacea for all the world's ills that they have no time and no capacity to analyze the ills and apply the balm accordingly.

The real question which we are confronting is whether our ministers shall have an adequate education or not. The good brethren who criticize Elmhurst do so under the guise of a defense of a classical against a scientific education, but they are really afraid of education in general. We are told on the one hand that it will dampen spiritual enthusiasm and cause men to bring matters extraneous to the gospel to the pulpit, and on the other hand the fear is expressed that many young men will decide to enter other callings once they are subject to the broadening influence of a college education. If there is nothing in the ministry that will appeal to educated young men and if we can force the choice of this profession upon them only by withholding other possible choices from them the church is in a more sorry state than most of us thought.

Perhaps the most impossible of all arguments against the development of our colleges is the charge that we were "aping the Yankees." Since when is a good college education an exclu-

SHALL A MINISTER HAVE AN EDUCATION?

sively American achievement?[4] Is the good professor not aware that it is not long since that we had an almost abject respect for any man among us who came from Germany with an "Universitaetsbildung" and picked our professors only from among those who had such an education? It is a sorry testimony for the hybrid nature of German-American culture that German-American denominations in America should be the only ones who do not offer their future ministers a college education before sending them to a theological seminary (not all American ministers have a college education, but all denominations offer the opportunity of securing one), while Germany is noted for her educational institutions. The German educational system has no exact equivalent for our four year college between high school and professional school, but it is folly to assert that the German student hasn't more than our junior college education when he takes up his professional studies. At any rate our complacency with our sublimated mission schools (for our two seminaries still bear traces of their mission school origin) is very discouraging, and the attempt to defeat the cause of higher education by appealing to war born prejudices against American institutions is conceived in ignorance and is more than discouraging. If it prevails we will always play a negligible part in American religious life.

---

[4]Mayer was particularly strong in his criticism: "We have aped the Yankees long enough" (Wir haben den Yankees lange genug nachgeäfft.). And to demonstrate the danger of such a course Mayer quoted Henry van Dyke, "I thank God that I don't know German." See Mayer, *op. cit.*, p. 91.

[As a result of his crucial 1923 summer in Europe, Niebuhr wrote a series of five articles, all of which are included here, for *The Evangelical Herald*. The first of these appeared on August 9, 1923.]

17. A Trip Through the Ruhr

The eyes of all Europe are turned to the Ruhr. For Germany it is the great affliction; for France it is the consummation of dreams of vengeance and for England it is the final disillusionment of the hopes for a pacified continent. America is too far away to understand or to care very much; yet the readers of the *Herald* are vitally interested and might therefore be served by an account of a recent trip through the occupied area.

The writer made the journey in company with Dean W. Scarlett, of Christ Church Cathedral, St. Louis, and Mr. Kirby Page, of the Fellowship for a Christian Social Order.[1] We entered the Ruhr at Dortmund after discovering that it was impossible to enter by way of Wesel and Duisburg, where the Germans had recently blown a bridge and the French had offered reprisals in the form of complete stoppage to traffic. The French lines are drawn in Brackel, a suburb of Dortmund. They are formed by barbed wire entanglements defended by soldiers. No German is allowed to pass them since the Duisburg disaster.

The Ruhr is completely separated from the rest of Germany

---

[1] Niebuhr, Scarlett and Page were among some fifty members of the third so-called "American Seminar" under the leadership of Sherwood Eddy. The purpose of these annual study groups was to acquaint a specially-selected group of educators and lecturers with events in Europe by meeting the leaders of those countries. For a more complete discussion of the Seminars see Sherwood Eddy, *Eighty Adventurous Years: An Autobiography*. New York: Harper & Brothers, 1955, pp. 128-151.

A TRIP THROUGH THE RUHR

and there were rumors about that the two weeks "Verkehrssperre" (blockade) would be extended from time to time to make this isolation permanent. Because of our American passports we however had no difficulty in entering. The right of entrance was taken so suddenly from Germans that many families were separated and wives and husbands and mothers and children were calling to each other over the barrier about family affairs. Only death in the family permits their reunion.

The great industrial city of Dortmund shows hundreds of idle smoke stacks. The great mines are closed because the French have levied a tax on the coal produced which the Germans refuse to pay and German workmen refuse to work the mines taken over by French soldiers. The city is quiet and French soldiers are stationed everywhere. The best hotels are occupied by them and children are on half-time because the schools are also used as barracks. The atmosphere is tense and unpleasant. French soldiers are left severely alone. Germans avert their faces as they parade down the street. The railroads are run by French soldiers. Train service is infrequent because Germans refuse to ride on the French trains.

After inspecting Dortmund we went to Essen, one of the greatest industrial cities of the world. There we had an interview with the present head of the great Krupp organization. Five of the directors of this vast industrial establishment, employing over 50,000 men, are in prison for from ten to twenty years for alleged sabotage. This is in spite of the fact that Krupp is running full force, though it has no market for its goods. It will run for another two months, we were told, and after that this plant too must be closed.

How vital the Ruhr is to the economic life of Germany may be seen from the fact that it produces approximately eighty percent of the coal and iron needed by German industry and produces more than the whole nation of France. If France can detach this heart of industrial Germany she will have achieved the final dismemberment of her enemy and will have added vast natural resources to her own economic life. That this is the object of France is no longer doubted in Europe, not even in England. We purchased the French propaganda sheet "Die Rheinische Republik," filled with specious arguments for a detached Rhineland, which would naturally be brought under the shadow of France. Incidentally we had some difficulty in securing the paper. The German news dealers whom we asked for it repulsed us with ugly mien but one finally consented to tell us where it could be secured when we told him that we were Americans.

We asked one of the most prominent industrial leaders of the Ruhr whether there was any hope in the situation. He answered that there was a little hope; that what hope there was lay in the economic interests of Britain which still has an army of one and a half million unemployed, largely because her industry is affected by the Ruhr occupation.

This diagnosis seemed to be borne out by what we have seen in England. London papers, with the exception of the Northcliffe press, are unanimous against the Ruhr occupation and the whole country is getting increasingly anxious about it. To an American, accustomed to general indifference upon this vital question the atmosphere of London seems strange. Prime Minister Baldwin's statement in Commons yesterday (July 12) has been widely commented upon and generally approved. A war with France is not desired but everything short of that will be done to bring the French out of the Ruhr and bring the reparations problem to such an issue that it can be settled.

Men of the standing of Sir Gilbert Murray have told us that if the reparations problem could be placed into the hands of an

A TRIP THROUGH THE RUHR

impartial tribunal it could be settled in a fortnight. The Germans are probably ready to pay the equivalent of twelve billion gold marks and the bona fide reparations are impartially estimated at fifteen billion gold marks. The difference is not great enough to wreck Europe if the conscience of Europe can be brought to bear upon the problem. And Europe has a conscience, that is one of the hopeful signs that impresses a student of European affairs. There are men of good will in all the nations who are striving diligently and desperately to save European civilization from complete collapse.

In conclusion it might be interesting to revert to our trip and report that we went from Essen to Duesseldorf in a train crowded to suffocation with French soldiers in weather that has broken the heat records of Europe. From Duesseldorf we proceeded to Koeln, where the British army is in control and where evidences of prosperity and good will are in marked contrast to the atmosphere of the rest of the Rhineland. Incidentally we heard on very good authority that British troops are still on the continent because of the definitely expressed wish of the Germans that they remain, and that the departure of American troops from Koblenz is everywhere regretted. The benevolent occupation of our "doughboys" has been superseded by the usual French severity.

In Koeln we feasted our eyes on the beautiful cathedral and attended mass there on Sunday morning. A Dominican monk preached to 9,000 people, but meanwhile the railroad station was crowded with hundreds of young people belonging to the "youth bands" so widely developed in Germany. They are sporadic evidences of the revolt of youth against the atmosphere of despair which has gripped their elders. Communing with nature they try to forget their troubles.

We tried to forget ours and those of Europe by engaging aeroplane passage and flying from Koeln to London in three hours.

[From *The Evangelical Herald*, September 13, 1923.]

18. Germany in Despair

A casual visit to Germany is not a pleasure jaunt, for whatever purpose it may have been undertaken, if the person who makes it has any semblance of feeling in his heart. For what he witnesses here is the very death throes of the once great nation. Such a statement will seem severe to Americans, who in spite of every report from the other side can not really imagine the desperation of Germany today; but here in Berlin (Aug. 9) it is being taken for granted that the end has come. Germans have exhausted their spiritual resources in hoping against hope and now the great majority hope no more. The preacher in the great "Dom" of Berlin, which we attended yesterday, spoke sadly and truly of the "arrogant unbelief and pitiful despair" of the German people.

That Germany is sick we have long known. But now the Ruhr invasion has opened the jugular vein of the patient and seems to make his recovery impossible. The terrible depreciation of the mark is caused by the heavy purchases of foreign coal by German industries, made necessary by the cutting off of the supply of coal from the Ruhr which formerly produced seventy per cent of the German coal. Furthermore, the feeling of the nation that Germany will not recover is an additional cause of the fall of the mark, which Germany must sell in order to gain imports, and which no one wants to buy. Since we entered Germany the mark has fallen from 200,000 to the dollar until now we buy one million marks for an American dollar. The results of this depreciation are grotesque. A pound of butter costs more than a day's wages, and a pair of shoes more than a month's salary. Housemaids receive the equivalent of 40 cents per month and skilled workers about four cents per hour. There is no unemployment but Germany has become the sweatshop of the world.

GERMANY IN DESPAIR

These economic facts are driving the workers to desperation and they are falling prey to communistic propaganda which every day is gaining converts from the ranks of the saner socialistic parties. The tension between extreme nationalists and extreme communists is becoming daily more acute. Today the general secretary of the Trade Union Congress estimated that one-fourth of the trade union members were communists. And the desperation of hunger is daily driving thousands to the ranks of communism. Not only the class spirit but national particularism is threatening to break up the unity of the Empire. There is a movement in Bavaria to unite with Austria and form a Catholic monarchy under the house of Wittelsbach. The separatist movement in the Rhineland is carefully nursed by the French government, though it must be stated that it does not appeal to very many. We were roughly treated when we tried to buy the French propaganda paper, "Die Rheinische Republik." Yet forces of disintegration are everywhere mainfest.

The disintegration of the political unity and economic vitality of Germany is however not as tragic as the disintegration of its moral life. The years of war and now the long years of anxiety which the peace has brought have totally unnerved these once solid, not to say stolid people. The literature on the newsstands of Berlin is predominatingly neurotic in character and religious leaders speak sadly of the breakdown of the general morale. In this morning's paper it is lamented that thieves are robbing cemeteries of everything movable. Hotels frantically admonish you to leave nothing outside your rooms, lest it be taken. This does not mean that the morality of all Germans has markedly deteriorated, but it does mean that the general moral standards of a people once noted for their moral robustness have sadly depreciated. No American can picture to himself the sadness of Germany, the tension of her political life, the hopeless despair which is gradusually engulfing her. There seems to be no cause for hope.

As a matter of fact, the only hope of Germany is America.

Both England and Germany are agreed in this. England and America are the only two countries who are anxious for international health on the continent of Europe. They are the only nations who are not animated by motives of revenge. But England is practically powerless because America has withdrawn from European affairs and has left the continent to the tender mercies of French chauvinism. The Germans have long since ceased to hope for help. Yet in spite of themselves they hope against hope. This is proven by the fact that German papers are anxiously scanning the political horizon of America to see if the death of President Harding might bring a change from the policy of isolation.

They have rightly concluded that it will not do so and are returning to this attitude of hopelessness. There is no sign on the political sky that would warrant any faith in aid from the outside world. That there are Germans who nevertheless believe that their country will be saved goes without saying. There are Christian Germans whose faith, challenged by the desperate situation in which they find themselves, has been purified and refined so that it bears many resemblances to the religion of the prophets. There are liberal circles in Germany who have not ceased to hope for reconciliation with France. They feel sure that if the best in Germany can find contact with the best in France the problems which produce hatred between the two countries can be easily settled. As a matter of fact, it is interesting that the workers of France, England and Germany have had many meetings, and have come to a complete agreement not only on the question of reparations but on the whole problem of Europe and believe that if given more power they could bring peace to Europe.

The German workers believe it would be easy to become reconciled with France if the French workers were more powerful. It must be admitted that the French political parties who are

GERMANY IN DESPAIR

working for a reconciliation number almost one-third of the French chamber of deputies. But the two-third majority of Poincare ruthlessly overrides every opposition and the French press hardly intimates that such opposition exists. Whatever the forces of liberalism are, they are not sufficient to save the immediate situation.

Humanly speaking, there seems no hope for Germany. Disaster seems to face her. She will not capitulate until forced to do so by starvation. The indications are that starvation will force her to capitulate in the Ruhr some time this winter. Yet farsighted Germans point out that this will be only an incident in the real problem; for one defeat will lead to new demands on the part of the enemy. At a meeting called by the "Social Science Club" of Berlin last night, which we had the privilege of attending, a well-known professor put the real problem in all its seriousness when he said: "Whatever the immediate circumstances may be, they are incidental. The real problem is, how can Germany and France be reconciled. If the best elements of both nations do not work for the consummation of that end we shall ultimately perish together and prove the complete bankruptcy of modern civilization."

[From *The Evangelical Herald*, September 20, 1923.]

19. The Despair of Europe

"What is the way out?" is the inevitable question an American asks a European when he comes in close contact with the desperate situation in which Europe finds herself. Whether in London or Berlin, he gets strikingly similar answers. One is told "That is a typical American question. You Americans are born optimists. You always think there is a way out. This time there is none. Europe is doomed."

This pessimistic conclusion is common in every part of Europe. In varying degrees of despair the intellectual world believes that the present European situation spells the breakdown of modern industrial civilization. Some think it might have been averted by various policies; *if* Wilson had had the statesmanship to support his idealism; *if* Lloyd George had had as much conscience as he had dexterity; *if* America had not been so ignorant of European politics and had not sacrificed her interest in Europe immediately after the war; *if* the Allies had not completely disarmed Germany, and a dozen other "ifs" give food for more or less hopeless speculation.

There are others who go deeper in their pessimism and declare that the modern industrial world which was built up in the 19th century was bound to perish in such a catastrophe as now seems imminent. Its artificialities, the hundred million people of Europe who are divorced from the soil and live in highly complex urban centers where they must vie for their living with the industrial workers of other nations who also are dependent upon world trade for their living, the animosities which are created by this struggle—all this was ultimately bound to result in disaster.

THE DESPAIR OF EUROPE

Against these voices of despair there are still some messages of hope. The churches on the whole have a desperate but rather confused hope. They think that somehow or other God will bring good out of evil but they seem to be hemmed in by a thousand traditions when they are called upon to support the forces of international conciliation. There are others, generally the forces of labor and political liberalism, who think that Europe could be saved if only the liberal influences of all nations could unite and create a new order in which forgiveness would prevail over hate and vengeance.

But all this seems terribly remote in the face of the present situation. Will any force of church, labor or intellectual liberalism be able to do anything before the new militarism of France completely wrecks the life of Europe? That is the question that every observer of European life must ask himself. On the face of it there seems to be no hopeful answer possible to this question. France is talking about reparations, but she is talking and talking because she knows that the complete disintegration of Germany is imminent and she hopes it will be accomplished while she parries the thrusts of England in fruitless debate.

The disintegration of Germany is a vague word and it might be well to vivify it by talking about possibilities. Germany may disintegrate by the complete disorganization of her economic life, which will result in widespread unemployment, the ravages of which the German people have no reserve to meet. It may mean communist uprisings caused by the desperation of hunger, and offering the French a pretext for violating the independence of Germany even further under the guise of restoring order.

France can not, of course, hope to occupy Germany permanently. What she wants above all is not the economic but the political ruin of the German state. And that, too, seems imminent. There are strong possibilities that Bavaria will seek to separate from Germany and organize a conservative monarchy under the house of Wittelsbach. There are possibilities that Saxony and Thuringia will seek to establish a completely socialist state. And while the Rhineland is more loyal than the states already mentioned, there is a chance that the French propagandists may build up a Rhenish republic under the protection of France against which German loyalty might battle in vain for many a year.

All this is possible. It is possible too that the French will completely annex the Ruhr and with the coke of the Ruhr and the iron of Lorraine will be able to defy the rest of Europe, England included, both in the industrial and in the military sphere. There are Germans who think that this all is inevitable. There are many Englishmen who think so, too.

Yet there are some rays of light. They are not many but they should not be despised. There is the fact that England is beginning to guide the whole conscience of Europe against this aggression. Most of the neutral states are in sympathy with her. France has on her side only the states whose armies she is supporting by her own funds. England will not fight France. She is too sick of war to do that, and it is well that she will not. Another war would be the sure death throe of modern civilization. But the moral influence of all these nations isolating France is tremendous.

There is a chance also, though a very slim one, that passive resistance may succeed; and if it does, it will mark one of history's greatest moral advances. There is a chance that the Poincare government will fall and that the one-third minority in the French house of deputies under Painleve may come into power. The outside world never hears of this minority but it exists and its power is not inconsiderable. There is a chance that the Stresemann government will bring order out of chaos at home

THE DESPAIR OF EUROPE

and start some effort of concilation with France. The Stresemann government represents a combination of the "Volkspartei" and of the social democratic party, a union, in other words, of the great industrialists and the industrial workers of Germany. That union is significant. It represents forces which have been more interested in their political theories and their economic advantages than in the preservation of their fatherland. Their union, though temporary, spells a change of heart.

The policy of the Stresemann government can be summed up in one sentence. It is: We will sacrifice, if we must, the autonomy of German industry in order to save the autonomy of the German state. That is a heroic policy and it may succeed, though disintegration may be too far advanced for any policy to succeed, and the purposes of France *may* be too mad for any heroism to challenge it.

There is a chance—would to God that it were a better one—that America will cease to wipe her hands in innocency and assume the responsibility for European conditions which her participation in the war makes inevitable. English and Germans on every hand insist that American participation in European affairs is the only hope. If the late notes of the British government had been joint notes with America, and if the economic power of the two only creditor nations were solidly behind them a different story would already be unfolding in Europe. Politically speaking, American participation is the only chance. We are not better than European nations, but we have no axes to grind in Europe. We have no virtue above Europe but we have good fortune, and if we were to exploit it morally we could save Europe.

Yet, finally, Europe's salvation must be achieved by more thoroughgoing forces than any political policy. Europe must learn to overcome its hate and learn the divine art of forgiveness. Europe must realize that the whole war was a satanic blasphemy against God and that nations must not only ask forgiveness of each other but must ask God to forgive them. Europe must learn that you can only forgive an enemy by doing the foolish thing and trusting him beyond his deserts, whereupon, as every experience proves, he will justify your faith beyond its expectations. That is after all the whole Gospel of Jesus. The world does not believe it. The churches do not believe it. If they believed it sincerely and robustly they could save Europe and our whole civilization in a generation.

Europe is in despair. It has good cause to be. Her doom is impending and she refuses to rise to the faith which alone could save her from disaster.

[From *The Evangelical Herald,* October 11, 1923.]

20. The Youth Movement of Germany

Visiting the city of Cologne and engaging rooms at a hotel in the very shadow of the great Cologne cathedral, the writer was awakened one Sunday morning by the tramp of many feet and the singing of weird old songs accompanied by banjo and guitar. Upon investigation the singing was found to come from bands of young people twenty to thirty in number. After several had passed down the street our curiosity overcame our Sunday morning lethargy and we dressed hurriedly to follow the young people down the street. We found them congregated by the hundreds in the railroad station ready for an "Ausflug" (outing). Young men and women aged fifteen to eighteen, the young men dressed in quaint costume of decorated hat, brown shirt, short leather trousers and sandals, the young women wearing dresses that reminded one of ancient lithographs remembered out of childhood, were mixing in joyful and free comradship. This was the "youth movement" of Germany mobilized.

Every city of the nation can present similar sights on Saturday and Sunday. For one of the characteristics of the youth movement is its love of nature. It started as a protest against the artificialities of the modern industrial and urban life and "back to nature" is one article in its creeds. Thousands of the young people of Germany are thus using their week-ends, and some times a whole week, to escape the conventional life of the city and to seek freedom under God's open sky. Every one wears a knapsack. After the manner of our own Boy Scouts, everyone has learned to cook with a minimum of kitchen tools, and tanned limbs give evidence that the experience is not a new one for any of the band.

Arrived in the country the bands spend their time in joyful

abandon and meditative communing with nature. If it is a Christian youth band the day will be begun with a simple devotional led by a few of the young men or women themselves. The afternoon will be spent in dance. But it is not the modern dance. The youth movement has turned its face against the indecencies of the modern dance. It has revived the old folk dances just as it relearned the old folk songs. It voices a virile and robust protest against the sickly sentimentalities of the modern song and against the poorly concealed indecencies of the modern dance. But the protest is not a Puritan one. The young men bid you to notice this fact, for they have no patience with Puritanism. They do not repress, they try to transfigure. The youth movement of Germany represents a significant balance of the natural buoyancy of youth and its awakening sense of responsibility. There is a serious note in it but not a morbid one. There is a joyful atmosphere about it but not a licentious one.

Whatever may be the sins of the adults of Germany, the youth movement is definite proof of the moral advantages which the young people of Germany possess over the young people of America. Sex morality has undoubtedly been cleaner in America than in modern Germany. But tables seem to be turning. The young people of America are sacrificing the standards of the fathers with a gay abandon that sickens the heart of every careful observer. In Germany the youth have turned against indecency and they have done so spontaneously. The youth movement of Germany is not a carefully nurtured organization under the tutelage of adults, as so many C. S's. and Y.M.C.A.'s in America are. It is a spontaneous revolt of the young peeople themselves against the impurities of modern life. Sometimes its insistence of a single standard of morals has tended to bring the higher standard down to the lower and the free intercourse of the sexes particularly in the inevitable hikes is not without its dangers, that has in isolated bands produced very regrettable erotic tendencies. But the movement on the whole has always had the sanity and the courage to cleanse itself of these weaknesses.

Yet the movement is not primarily a revolt against impurity. It is primarily a revolt against the conventionality and insincerity of modern life. It is a revolt against traditional patriotism with its inevitable reverse side of hatred against other peoples. Some of the youth bands are definitely pacifistic. It is a revolt against traditional pedagogy which in Germany meant a complete lack of fellowship between teacher and scholar, and a relationship of mutual distrust and incipient conflict between them. It is trying to substitute love for respect and fellowship for formal authority. It is a revolt against the national family customs in particular against the continental autocracy of the father. The young men refuse to have either their wives or their careers picked for them by their parents, as has been so common all over Europe. It is a revolt against a traditional piety that repeats ancient creeds and formularies and puts no breath of spiritual insight into modern life.

All this is so spontaneous and is propelled so much by the initiative of the young people themselves that one is bound to estimate the movement as one of the rays of light that penetrate the darkness of modern Europe. Where young people can combine youthful exuberance with serious concern for the future of their civilization, and where they can make earnest efforts to challenge the worst and resurrect the best in the history of their people, one need not despair. Germany is in the very winter of her discontent, but the youth movement is the harbinger of spring.

Any movement that revolts so energetically against old traditions and conventionalities is bound to be tempted to destroy some of the finer achievements which lie embodied in these forms. The youth movement has not been free of this temptation. Impatience with military orderliness has sometimes led to disorderly life; revolt against unjustified parental control can easily degenerate into unwarranted disobedience; scorn of the barren conventionalities of religion can easily drive the youth into the camp of irreligion. All this has happened among the young people of Germany, but the youth movement has a main stream of pure and robust idealism that augurs well for the future of the nation.

The original movement bearing the name "Wandervoegel" (birds of passage) was non-sectarian and non-political and it resisted every effort to capture it for any particular religious or political tendency. Nevertheless, there are now youth bands under the auspices of various political and religious organizations. The Catholics have appropriated a great deal from the youth movement for their young people's work. Protestant leaders like Paul Leseur have reanimated the young people's work of the Evangelical and Lutheran churches, and the Y. M. C. A. with the spirit of freedom, brotherhood and spontaneity which characterizes the movement. The Social Democrats and even the Communists have their own organizations of young people, and after the Jews were more or less excluded out of the original youth bands, they too have organized their own leagues.

While this diversity of adult interest has diversified the aims and purposes of the youth bands there is nevertheless an undeniable relationship of spirit and atmosphere in all of them. One might characterize it as a revolt against complacency. The young people of Europe are not going to accept civilization from their elders without inquiring into it. They are not going to swallow the bitter with the sweet. They are going to probe and investigate and aspire. They are going to "hunger and thirst" after something finer and nobler than modern civilization seems to offer an idealist. They are the leaven in the lump of Europe.

[From *The Evangelical Herald*, November 1, 1932.]

21. America and Europe

America has withdrawn from Europe for two reasons. One is that we are too far away to know what is really happening over there, or to care even if we do know. The sense of responsibility is after all sharpened by proximity more than by any other single factor. The other is that we think Europe is going the way of destruction in spite of our well meant effort to help her in the late war. Selfishness and pharisaism, in other words, are the two sins of America in relation to Europe.

It is true we are far away and a great ocean separates us from the turmoil of the continent. Yet the late war taught us how intertwined are the destinies of nations and how civilization has become one woof and warp. For a time we may be able to preserve our prosperity while Europe is poor but in the long run even the economic life of the world is going to prove to us that God created us to be one and that no nation liveth to itself alone. If Europe will continue poor we will ultimately be poor. If civilization perishes in Europe our civilization will finally perish with it. We are spiritually a part of Europe. Our favored geographic position may save us for a time from the fate of European civilization, but it can not save us in the long run.

But physical isolation is not the only cause of our moral withdrawal from Europe. The real spiritual cause of the withdrawal seems to be a feeling that Europe is not worthy of our aid. We reason very naively that we tried to help her once to establish peace and since she seems to have scorned our good purposes we will make up our mind to have nothing to do with her. The best answer to this seemingly plausible argument is that it is our very withdrawal from Europe which has made it possible for the evil forces of Europe to exploit the Allied victory.

An under-secretary in one of the German ministries analyzed the situation to the writer as follows: "America thrice intervened in the affairs of Europe in the last years. The first time was when she came into the war and made Allied victory possible. If she had not come the war would have resulted in a stalemate. The second time was when Wilson's policies prevented the French from exploiting the victory in the way they expected to. We Germans have never appreciated this part until now. For the peace was so contrary to the Fourteen Points that we did not realize that it was also out of harmony with the real war aims of France. The third intervention was American withdrawal from Europe, which made it possible for the French to do belatedly what they intended to do in the beginning. Had it not been for the stubborn resistance of England and America France would have been in the Rhur in the very beginning.

This exposition seems fair and accurate and reveals the tremendous responsibility of America. We helped to create the conditions which agitate the life of Europe today, and our pharisaic withdrawal makes them even more intolerable.

The anniversary of the Armistice five years ago should force us to ponder these facts very seriously. We should assume our share of responsibility for Europe which is pressed upon us not only by the spiritual ideal of the unity of the human race but by the specific fact that we helped to create the conditions which we deplore.

But what shall we do? What *can* we do not to make confusion worse confounded? The answer to this question is not really as difficult as it seems.

First of all, we should insist on the revision of the treaty. In England there is an almost unanimous sentiment that the treaty ought to be revised. Years ago Prof. Keynes began the agitation for the revision of the treaty. Just recently the British Quakers published a brilliantly thought out document calling for revision of the treaty. The great English labor party is equally insistent that the treaty be revised. Britain has the support of most of the neutral nations in this demand. She lacks only the support of America. We are not interested.

And our lack of interest is water on the French mill. France will do what she wants to do in Europe as long as we do not come to the aid of the sane opinion in Europe. Anyone who thinks that Europe has gone completely mad does not know the facts. In every country there are forces of righteousness at work, anxious to contribute something to the conciliation of the nations.

While American cooperation need not come by way of the League of Nations it is a fact that the League is an instrument of French policy largely because we are not in it. The writer went to Europe a confirmed enemy of the League but came back in a chastened mood. All the best forces in Europe are for it. German liberal leaders expressed great surprise that liberal forces in America are opposed to it. However, the League is involved in so many internal political difficulties in America that a friend of peace will not stress this point. There are a dozen ways for America to say that she will not be party to the policies which are now devastating Europe. She need not use the League in order to help Europe.

Then we must make concessions in regard to war debts. The first question that would confront any conference which tried to revise the treaty would be the matter of reparations. Everyone knows that the reparation claims of France are impossible. It is the case of one bankrupt trying to extort money out of another bankrupt. Yet it is a fact that France has spent more money on her devastated regions than German reparations have been able to pay. We will not get far with France, a poor nation, if we in our wealth, give her pious advice and nothing more.

What we ought to do is to confront France with the alternative of forcing her to pay her debt to us or forgiving her a portion of her debt to us, conditioned upon a reasonable attitude toward her foe. This is the policy that England has suggested several times. But every economic conference called for that purpose came to naught because of America's and France's failure to cooperate. France refused because she did not want to revise her reparation claims, and America refused because we were afraid we would be milked. If we maintain that kind of selfish attitude we have nothing to contribute to European convalescence. Her doom will be sealed by American selfishness.

Those who know the facts in regard to European conditions ought to do everything in their power to sting the American conscience and arouse it out of its present apathy. There are strong forces in Europe working for a better day. They are in despair chiefly because America will not aid them. And the curious thing is that some of our most liberal forces have helped to create this policy of isolation. It is time that we think straighter on this whole European issue and cease to strengthen the hands of those who are making the doom of European civilization inevitable.

["On Academic Vagabondage," at first glace appears to be rare Niebuhrian frivolity. Below the surface, however, this article, which was printed in the February, 1924 issue of *The Keryx*, contains a definite challenge to the readership to temper their Mid-Western German-American provincialism through continuing education at other educational institutions.]

22. On Academic Vagabondage

The writer hardly dares to classify himself as an academic vagabond. He took considerable pride in his record of attendance at eight colleges and seminaries including Eden and Elmhurst, until he met a man the other day with fifteen scholastic scalps dangling from his belt. Since then his mistaken conceit has taken refuge in aspirations and vague dreams of future wanderings. His limited experience, confined to the United States, does not permit him to assume the tone of authority, but only to speak with the modesty becoming to a novice of the benefits to be derived from academic hoboism, and to accept with meekness the corrections more hardened tramps will offer.

A primary advantage to be gained from attendance at a number of schools located in different parts of the country, is the effect of such a procedure upon one's provincialism. Most of us receive our education at schools whose students belong to a rather closely defined, homogeneous group. Our classmates were geographically, religiously, politically and racially our neighbors even before we met at collge. Our viewpoints tend to coincide. We share the peculiarities of temperament and outlook, good and bad, which characterize our section of the country, our religious denomination, our race. At Elmhurst and Eden we are almost all Middle-Western, German-American, Evangelical Synod folks. What is true of these schools is true in greater or less degree, and with appropriate change in the defining terms, of most small colleges and even of state-universities. Education under such conditions has its distinct advantages, but also its peculiar disadvantage. Academic vagabondage offers no substitute but an important complement to such undergraduate training.

The scholastic tramp who spends a semester at Columbia and Union, at Harvard, or Yale or Chicago, is thrown into contact with men and women from the most widely separated sections of the continent and of the world, from all sorts of religious groups, with representatives of various races. He must perforce revise his theories as to the characteristics of Methodism, of the Baptist and the Unitarians; he notes that the Hindu, the Chinaman and the son of Nippon are very much like himself; he discovers some things about the spirit and meaning of their political forms and their religious beliefs which text-books never had or could have taught him. During the past year there was at Yale a more or less fluctuating group of graduate students brought together by the initial tie of a common love for My Lady Nicotine, I believe, or by a common admiration for a certain professor, which included an Australian who had gone to college in Columbia, Mo., and Eureka, Ill., and had lived two years in Russia, a Hindu who had brought with him from Edinburgh a Scotch burr and from Oxford an English *a*, a South African Boer with a French name, a Chinaman with Princeton training, and two Americans from the Middle-West, one of whom qualified for admission to this international pot-pourri by his marriage to a French girl, the other by his indubitable German ancestry. To provide local color there were two Massachusetts Yankees. Denominationally the group was composed of Disciples, Congregationalists, Lutherans, Methodists, Church of England, etc. The merciless criticisms and mutual appreciation of each other's countries, national spirits, creeds, religious viewpoints and habits of thought were probably more helpful and salutary than much reading or an extended lecture course upon questions of international and interdenominational accord could have been. Many a pet prejudice was lost; many a new appreciation gained.

I have known similar groups at other institutions. There was a class in Chicago which brought together Jews, Jewesses, Chinese, Japanese and Koreans, missionaries home from Africa, high and low caste Hindus, Christian Scientists, Missouri Lutherans, etc. A non-theological touch was provided to that summer's work by an engineering student who lived across the hall and possessed an I. W. W. card, much more or less attractive information about the habits of seasonal workers in the wheat fields, and wild yarns about trips on cattle-boats across the Atlantic. To anyone who has missed that part of education which is supplied by such various contacts, a course in academic vagabonding is to be recommended or prescribed.

While we are discussing this subject of provincialism and its cure it is well to remember the considerable provincialism of the Mid-West in its attitude toward the East and the limitation of the Easterner's knowledge and judgment as to Western and Mid-Western character and conditions. There is for instance the popular superstition in which many of us were nurtured, regarding Yankee temperament and habits. Every Middle-Westerner knows that the New England Yankee is cold, shrewd, self-satisfied, supercilious toward all other races, and immensely proud of his Puritan ancestry. When that Middle-Westerner comes East and finds the sort of person he has had in mind, he is likely to make the disconcerting discovery that the Yankee's name is Ciaburro or Schmidt. I have lived in a Yankee village for more than a year, preaching in a Yankee church during that time, and I have found no kindlier, more generous and modest people than these New Englanders. Some of them are proud of their ancestors, it is true; so are some Middle-Westerners no doubt.

The Easterner has similar prejudices and false ideas about us of the Mississippi Valley. It is interesting these days to compare Nebraska's idea of New York with New York's idea of Nebraska. What a bugaboo Wall Street is in the Dakotas; what an inconceivable mystery the election of Magnus Johnston is in Connecticut! Insofar as the colleges are concerned, it is well-known in the west that Harvard and Yale are undemocratic, open only to rich men's sons; it is an established fact in the East that all Western schools are mere fresh-water colleges and that no student learns anything in our co-educational universities except love-making. It was related and believed by faculty members at an Eastern school that the adoration of Leland Stanford, Jr., at the university erected to commemorate him had gone so far as to cause the inclusion of a wax replica of Stanford's last meal among the museum treasures of the school. An academic tramp found out the truth behind the tale; in the museum at Stanford University there is a stone which in shape and color resembles a fried egg; hence the whole elaborate yarn. Such notions are not only childish, they contain an element of danger for our nation. Once before two sections of the country failed to understand each other. Scholastic vagabonding helps a little toward better mutual understanding.

The greatest advantage, of course, to be gained from a variegated college career is not to be sought in these incidental by-products but in the benefit derivable from instruction and instructors at various schools. No college has a monopoly of great teachers. Some schools excel in one department, some in another. An ideal school from the theological student's viewpoint would have on its faculty Harvard's philosophers and historian of religion, Yale's theologians, Union's and Teacher's historians, practical theologians and specialists in religious education, New Testament and social Christianity, and a Chicagoan or two to add spice. But since the mountain will not come to Mohammed, Mohammed must go to the mountain. Great teachers are as

ON ACADEMIC VAGABONDAGE

scarce as great preachers or great physicians and it is well worth while to journey a long way to find one. Beside the few great ones there are of course very many good ones everywhere, who only lack the spark of genius; these also one must hear; and often it is the less well-known instructor, whose course one chose as a filler, who bestows the richest treasures and kindles the most enduring enthusiasms.

Finally the academic tramp learns to know and to appreciate the various religious and scientific tendencies and moods which each have their representatives in the colleges and seminaries. The youthful, thoroughly American, pragmatic temper of Chicago—sometimes a little strident in its utterance—the warm personal piety of Yale—sometimes almost quietistic—the ripe scholarship and moral earnestness of Union with its fine sense for the social mission of our faith—all these have their place in the Christian life and in the theologian's thought. It's well worth while to go vagabonding from school to school to discover how various and how rich may be the expression of Christianity.

Such are some of the lures of academic tramping. Indulgence in this Wanderlust has its dangers of course. A rolling stone gathers no moss and the perpetually peregrinating pursuer of truth may find himself in the end less well-equipped with the moss of learning than is his more sedentary brother. But the rolling stone loses many a corner and jagged edge in his tumbling. And that's something too. For that matter a bird of passage can be detained by no arguments. The academic hobo joins his brother of the open road in the confession,
>"For to admire and for to see
>For to roam this world so wide,—
>It never done no good to me;
>But I can't stop it if I tried,"

and lays his plans for future wanderings. There is no limit to the voyages which may be projected. If American universities no longer tempt there are Oxford and Edinburgh, Cambridge and London, Berlin, Leipzig, Halle and Heidelberg, Goettingen, Tuebingen, Marburg and Bonn, Paris and the Sorbonne—delightful names to roll upon one's tongue—magic words with which to conjure up splendid day-dreams when the present palls. And when the academic tramp perforce must settle down to earn his daily bread what happy hours he can spend perusing catalogues and studying time-schedules of schools he has visited or never seen. Even old age won't rob him of those pleasures nor of his memories.

[In the summer of 1924 Niebuhr again went to Europe with the American Seminar during which time he contributed the following three articles exclusively to *The Evangelical Herald*. The first of these ran in the August 7, 1924 issue.]

23. The Dawn in Europe

Last year the situation in Europe was black without a touch of hope or light. Today there are faint glimmerings of a dawn. The forces that are to rebuild Europe seem actually to have begun work. Three factors have brought Europe hope. The advent of the Labor government in England, the experts' report on Reparations, and the fall of Poincare.

The confidence which England, not to say Europe, has gained in Ramsay MacDonald is hardly to be believed. His diplomacy undoubtedly has helped to develop a slightly saner attitude in France and contributed to the defeat of Poincare. His success in securing French consent for an allied conference to put the Dawes report into effect is another personal triumph and a victory for peace. The rise to power and prestige of this man is a romance more wonderful than anything found in fiction. Not to speak of his privations when he came to London, a poor Scotch lad of 19, one has only to think of his status during the war to gain some appreciation of what this life means. The head of the British Labor party in 1914, he resigned his leadership rather than participate in the war, whereupon he was defeated and lost even his seat in the House and twice failed when he attempted to come back. Finally in 1923 he was returned and now the man who was the best hated man in England is in the very center of the European stage and the hope of restoration in Europe. I could hardly believe my eyes when I read an editorial in the *London News* tonight, pleading with his friends to persuade him to conserve his health more carefully. This is one of the papers which only four short years ago bitterly reviled him; now it finds his health a national asset.

The defeat of Poincare is another omen of a better day in Europe. Not too much can be expected of Herriot but he is at least not a hopeless imperialist. Undoubtedly he would like to go further than he is actually now daring, but French public opinion will not permit. The mere suggestion that the new European conference might set up a body other than France's beloved Reparation Commission almost caused his down-fall and sent MacDonald pell mell to Paris to patch up some compromise whereby he could be saved. The compromise decided upon was to leave the Dawes report in the hands of the Reparation Commission with the promise that America is to be asked to add a member to this Commission. One wonders whether the Coolidge administration, in the midst of an election campaign, will have the courage to do this. The difficulty of an honest French statesman arises out of the fact that France has been fed on lies so long that it is practically impossible to tell her the truth. France is in fact a bankrupt nation with debts totaling 90 percent of all her real resources. She maintains herself only by the delusion of impossible reparation payments. Anything that destroys this delusion would result in nothing very short of a revolution, and a French statesman even of the radical school may therefore be pardoned for hesitating here.

This is the fact which explains the anomaly of the Dawes report. In many American circles it is foolishly taken for granted that this report finally settles the reparation problem. Of course such a conclusion is based upon ignorance. The Dawes report still demands the impossible sum of 33 billion dollars from Germany. If it can be enforced, it means the perpetual economic servitude of Germany. Its disadvantage is that it created in many ignorant minds the belief that this sum is actual and possible of payment. It therefore lays the foundation for fresh

THE DAWN IN EUROPE

charges of insincerity against Germany. But on the other hand it restores the economic unity of Germany and is the only step short of war which will get France out of the Ruhr. Furthermore, it takes the reparation problem out of the realm of the ephemeral and declares specifically where the money is to come from if it is to be paid at all. It clearly proves that Germany can pay reparations only if she exports more than she imports by some 200 to 500 million dollars a year. Inasmuch as Germany was not able to do this even before the war it may be seen how hopeless the situation is from this angle.

[From *The Evangelical Herald*, September 18, 1924.]

24. Berlin Notes

Impressions of an American In the German Capital

Today (it is August 11) the bands are playing and soldiers are marching. No, my companion informs me the marchers are not soldiers but police. They look like the traditional German soldiers with their patent leather helmets. The occasion is the fifth anniversary of the Weimar constitution which laid the foundation for the German republic. Thousands gather in the gardens before the palace where once the Hohenzollerns held forth. The window from which the Kaiser addressed his cheering subjects at the outbreak of the war is now filled with eager sightseers who got into the palace before the demonstrations began.

The president of the republic reviews the parade of police. They are followed by thousands of young men belonging to a recently organized "republican club" which calls itself "National flag: black, red, yellow." These are the republican colors everywhere in evidence today. The president addresses the multitude in a brief dignified speech. He speaks like a professor rather than a former saddler. One may judge from his remarks that the republic is not safe. It has bitter enemies to the right and to the left. A glance at the morning newspaper offers explanation for the president's solemn warnings.

There are millions of Germans who will have nothing of the republic. Their newspapers treat the day of anniversary with scorn. Yet it is probable that the republic has weathered the worst storms. Its enemies are not united and have no clear program. Furthermore, they know that any effort to restore the monarchy would plunge Germany into a bloody civil war. For the defenders of the republic are resolute and determined and are probably in the majority.

No wonder there are such varying reports on the loyalty of the German people to their churches. For one church is filled and the other well nigh empty. What is more, the same church may be crowded one week and forsaken the next, depending on the preacher. One gains the impression that churches are only preaching places over here, at least in the large cities. There is no week-day activity, no congregational life. Nothing in Europe compares to the intensive activity of the American church. Perhaps that is one of the fruits of the state church.

The dress of Berliners is visibly improved over that of last year and the zoological gardens are filled with eager crowds of merrymakers. They are just like American crowds except that they listen to a concert of Wagner instead of jazz rendered by the park band. Behind the scenes there are of course pictures of suffering. There is hardly a working family that can count on more than $25 per month. And unemployment is again increasing.

In other circles we have heard much of the suffering of the middle classes in Germany. Sometimes we have been led to believe that they suffer more than the working classes. Perhaps they do if mental anguish is taken into account. For thousands of families have been reduced from an easy competence to poverty. Yet I would like to dispute the general impression. No plight could be worse than that of the workingman who without reserves faces a winter of unemployment with nothing between his family and starvation but a dole of $10 to $12 a month. One marvels at the comparative patience of these people. History knows of revolutions which were bred in necessities less urgent than those which harass the German workingman. And there is no relief in sight for some years to come.

What a terrible toll was taken in the moral life of the people. Sex purity was once the pride of the German people. One wonders whether they can ever regain that claim. Perhaps the countrysides are still bulwarks of pure family life but the cities are corrupted with eroticism; street girls by the hundreds ply their ancient profession brazenly in every principal thoroughfare, and lascivious literature bedecks every newstand and book store. The little push carts from which books are sold on the street display the works of Schiller and Goethe on the same shelf with unmentionable titles which betray the diseased imagination. Yet there are those who spoke of the "cleansing fire of the war."

I can't find a Gothic church in Berlin. Perhaps there are one or two but most of the church architecture is Renaissance. It seems that the French influence on Frederick the Great left its indelible mark on the whole succeeding architecture of the city. This classic style of architecture is not imposing for churches. Is not the broken Gothic arch the permanent embodiment of the Christian idea, the most perfect symbol of the Christian faith?

[From *The Evangelical Herald*, September 25, 1924.]

25. Is Europe On the Way to Peace?

I have just returned (August 23) to London from a trip through the continent of Europe. Everywhere the attention of the nations was centered on the London Conference. American readers will hardly be able to realize how seriously this conference has affected the whole life of Europe and with what corresponding degree of anxiety and hope the peoples of Europe have followed its every move and analyzed its final results. The question everywhere is: Is this the turn in the road toward peace, or only another continuation of the war? For every previous peace conference has been merely a continuation of the old conflict and the common people have grown skeptical.

As far as I can see there is no conclusive answer to this question. It is being answered in both ways by various parties in the various countries. On the one hand there are those who are animated by a most extravagant optimism and predict that the London pact means a new day for Europe. They declare the peace of conciliation, which never took place at Versailles, now to be nearing fulfillment. In support of their hopes they certainly have a right to call attention to the fact that the London pact, whatever it may be, is better than anything which preceded it. It was made by three liberal governments who had defeated the extreme nationalistic movements in each one of their respective nations and represented the will to peace of their peoples. The old appeal to force and the atmosphere of distrust was absent from the conference. In place of it there was an evident intention to reach an agreement by each nation compromising some of its cherished interests. That concessions were actually made may be proven by the interesting fact that both Herriot and Marx presented the conference report to their respective chamber on the same day (Aug. 22) and each was violently and desperately opposed by the nationalist section of his parliament. This nationalist section represents in each country that portion which does not want to forget the war but takes an almost cruel delight in reopening the wounds at every opportunity. Yet on the whole each government seems to feel quite secure in its position against its nationalistic opposition.

On the other hand, the optimism which the London Conference has created is probably more extravagant than the facts warrant. In a sense it may be said that it has not improved on Versailles but has only mitigated the evils which were heaped on the injustices of Versailles. Germany is saved from immediate economic collapse and her economic unity is restored, both results which will make the acceptance of the London pact inevitable in Germany. But on the other hand, the nation has paid or will be forced to pay a very heavy price for the advantages. Her finances will be controlled, the independence of her railroads and her industries is sacrificed and a load is placed upon the German people almost too grievous to be borne. The German income is about $85 per capita per year. Taxes cut into this income to the extent of $30 per year, leaving but $55 per year for consumption. This low subsistence standard is to be further decreased by reparation payments which will cost almost $10 per capita, thus bringing the standard of living to a low level such as no civilized modern nation knows. The peace of Europe about which everyone speaks so optimistically must be paid for by workingmen, working 10 hours a day at the average wage of 10 cents per hour.

No wonder that the governments which are urging the acceptance of the Dawes plans must face not only nationalistic but communistic opposition, for the communists have grown strong on the argument that this "peace plan" is the plan of international finance to sweat the labor of 65 million people. This charge

IS EUROPE ON THE WAY TO PEACE?

is obviously without foundation. Bertrand Russell prophesied some time ago that Europe could be united only as a province of the finance power of the United States. America would march into Europe, put money behind its brains and its equipment, insist on peace as a prerequisite of profitable business and thus restore Europe even while it is enslaving it. The London Conference is actually the partial fulfillment of this prophecy. American bankers were actually the dominant elements of the London Conference and American money is to set Germany's wheels agoing again.

The need of gold-filled America for an outlet for its too exuberant resources explains the sudden departure from the policy of isolation, and under the leadership of the very party which not long since championed isolation is the A and O of political wisdom. This turn of events may well give pause to every American who is interested in seeing America serve the world. We are beginning to render that service but now, as since the world began, self-interest is the mainspring of our action. We are going to be peace-makers in Europe but also task-masters. Europe will love us for that and then hate us. We will guarantee the peace of Europe for the next few years. But whether politics built upon such foundations can really ensure a lasting peace may well be doubted.

["Our Educational Program," was delivered at the Fifth National Convention of the Evangelical Brotherhood which took place in East St. Louis, Illinois from September 14-17, 1924, where Niebuhr began to articulate his hope for the future role of the Church.]

26. Our Educational Program

I will be a little more orthodox than the brother that preceded me and will chose a text, the word of the Apostle: "Let your love grow more and more in all knowledge."[1]

I am to speak this evening on "Our Educational Program." I don't know why I was chosen to speak on this subject. I am afraid that we have not had any educational program. That is what is the matter with us. I have my own ideas as to what an educational program should be and this I want to represent to you tonight and hope that in the next years you will go and get together upon it. We have given very little consideration to education altogether. It is striking how the German-American gives the least consideration to it, when you see with what denials it is carried on in Germany even in these times, in spite of the poverty of the country. We wonder why the German-American lost his inheritance of his fathers.

In all the various Lutheran Synods we only find two or three large colleges. We ourselves have not risen to the standard of an A. B. College. We did not spend a penny for educational institutions in the years between 1890 and 1910. No new buildings went up in those 20 years. We have spent for these purposes in the

---

[1]The speaker preceding Niebuhr was Synod President John Baltzer who spoke on "The Synodical Outlook." Niebuhr, who had great admiration for Baltzer, was obviously joking in his reference to Baltzer's orthodoxy. Indeed, in their correspondence one clearly detects a warm personal relationship that frequently involved teasing.

last 10 years more money than in the entire history of our denomination. That would seem that we are gradually awaking. Yet thousands of our people have not yet caught a vision of the task even now. The conception of the majority concerning religious training is that it is only the training of ministers, not to train the educated Christian laymen. I remind you of the fact that we have not yet got a women's college, although we have enough places to have one. I hope that the Cincinnati school will soon grow to be a women's college, and a few other colleges should also be started. Some denominations as large as we are spending six times as much as we. They are not always taking the money out of the Sunday collection, but they are receiving large gifts from laymen for educational institutions. Buildings like gymnasiums by all means ought to be gifts. I could take you through the campuses of America and through many religious colleges, where you will find any number of buildings that were put there by interested laymen, men who are giving back part of what they and their ancestors had received. We ourselves started as a poor denomination and many who came to this country have received through our Church Christian fellowship and spiritual values. But we have not returned to the Church and education what we ought.

Religious Education Important

Religious education is so very important, because civilization seems to depend absolutely upon the task of welding religion with education. The power of goodwill must grow more and more in knowledge. We must bring religion and education together if we want to save civilization. Many people, especially in Europe, think that religion has lost its value as a power. One of the most read books in Europe today is Spengler's "Untergang des Abendlandes." I don't think we ought to be pessimistic to such an extent.

We do not realize that the civilization in which we are a part is a civilization in which we are to get along and to live with one another. And that this is a task of religion and a task of intelligence. We define civilization as the art of living together. We don't know how to divide what our modern civilization has produced, we don't know how to live together in spite of our riches. I believe religion has a real function to perform in helping people to live with one another. Some people say, human nature is selfish and brutal beyond help, but I think they are wrong. I believe we can change human nature with all its brutal and selfish instincts, first by religion, second by education. Because it has unlimited resources, it can be developed into something much finer than our imagination can conceive.

The Love Factor

Certainly it is more necessary that we live with one another than ever before. There are more than ever of us, we are living so close together, we are so interdependent, our modern civilization is so complex, that we need more love and more religion than ever before, in our complex social relationships. Our fathers could live by themselves on their farms, but our age is different. Love is becoming a more and more necessary factor to our civilization and we have to produce it. That is the business of religion. We are selfish by nature. We need not try to deny it. We all try and see how we can get the most. All life is selfish when it is not changed by some spiritual influence. Religion can change us. It challenges us that we are spiritual beings. Nothing else can make man more than a beast, religion can make him a child of God. Uncompromising sacramentalism is the only religion that can bring these changes about. But we have not learned yet what it means to be spiritual beings. Many do not know what it is to be spiritual themselves, a son of God. And many do not know how to treat the other man as a son of God.

OUR EDUCATIONAL PROGRAM

The civilization of Europe is corrupt because they have not had this sacramental vision of life. They have only had the natural materialistic conception of life instead of the spiritual. We must, first of all, have love. We must continually produce it by bringing people into fellowship with God. And because love is not enough, religion is not enough; love must be intelligent and religion must be educated. That is why I say we have not had a religious education. We must educate all fine instincts that religion breathes, as the Scripture says: "Let his mind be in you." Too many men have not the mind of Christ. Many people have a Christian heart but not a Christian mind. They do not think in a Christian way, and do not use their intelligence to create a Christian civilization. I believe in putting the Christian Church into politics, but I would not trust it to go into politics just now. It does not know enough, it is too ignorant. It takes into politics, not the mind of Christ, but its own little ideas and its own bigotries. A religion that divides men is not a real religion. A man that sets men against his brethren may be a willing Christian, but he has not the true religion. We are divided all the time by so much. Natural life is dividing us all the time. The purpose of religion is to unite us.

Self-Righteousness

In Germany I was talking this summer to a German pastor of the "Gemeinschaft". He was telling me how corrupt the Church was. He told me how his group was getting togther the truly converted believers, to unite their forces of prayer to help the terrible state of the German nation. When I asked him for his opinion of how he thought that was to be brought about, he said: "We must first get the Jews out of politics." All the fine Christian spirit that man possessed was corrupted by that kind of spirit. Here lie the great paradoxes in our modern civilization. These kind of people are ruining our world. If the world will go down, it will not go down by the hands of criminals, but by the hands of those that were so conscious of their righteousness.

If we are going to have a Christian civilization, we will have to have religion in the heart and in the mind. Religion must be intelligent. That is the business of the Christian Church. If we are not going to do the work, the world is going to crush us aside and go its own way.

[The little-known essay which appeared in a volume entitled *Preachers and Preaching in Detroit* edited by Ralph Milton Pierce and published by Fleming H. Revell Company in 1926, was Niebuhr's first article printed in book form. It is an excellent piece which concisely presented many of his Detroit learnings and is included here with the permission of the Fleming H. Revell Company.]

27. Tyrant Servants[1]

"The Sabbath was made for man and not man for the Sabbath." — MARK 2:27.

Man has a curious weakness for giving such unthinking devotion to the institutions and governments which are meant to serve him that he tempts them to assume arbitrary power over him and to conceive their life as an end in itself and not as a means to an end. Human history is filled with evidences of this curious perversity. Jesus encountered it in the institution of the Sabbath. Whatever motives of taboo may first have caused primitive man to set aside a holy day and the early Semite to keep the Sabbath, religion at its best and as the prophets interpreted it, justified the Sabbath for its social and human value as a day of rest and worship.

The Sabbath, according to the best Jewish thought, was made for man; but so great was the concern of the legalist for the keeping of the Sabbath and so great was the fear of the people that they might violate its sanctity that it became hedged about with a hundred and one laws calculated to enforce rest and quiet. These laws interfered so much with natural, wholesome and even necessary activities that to keep the Sabbath became a burden rather than a boon to man. Jesus, with that natural regard for the wholesome and natural and instinctive aversion

---

[1] Niebuhr was so little-known at this point that his name appeared throughout the article as "Neibuhr."

to artificialities which characterized His whole ministry, was in constant conflict with the Sabbath legalists.

At the present moment we are not interested in the immediate question of Sabbath observance, except to note that our own Puritanism is not always free of the sins which Jesus imputed to Sabbath legalists. What interests us is the wider tendency in human thought and action of which the Sabbath legalism is but a symptom and the wider implication of the principle for which Jesus contended. Institutions are made for men and not men for institutions. Except by constant and jealous vigiliance it is impossible to restrain the servants of mankind from becoming its tyrants.

The problem of keeping our servants in their proper place has been a vexing one throughout the history of civilization. Governments which were meant to bless human life with the virtues of social order have easily become the oppressors of men; religions which should have emancipated man from every tyranny elevated the priest into positions of irresponsible autocracy; mysteries such as those of man's sex life in which some of the best values of human life are enmeshed have become the occasion for degradation, as for instance in the phallic orgies of primitive religions. Nothing is so good and so useful but that it cannot be corrupted by excessive veneration. If it has been a problem throughout human history to observe a due sense of proportion in dealing with tools and means of human happiness, that problem is more urgent today than ever before. Human life is more social than it once was; and, therefore, the authorities which are the by-products of social order are more potent; life is more complex, and the institutions through which we express it have therefore become more difficult to control.

It is a real question in the modern day whether the nation has not become as much a foe as a servant of human happiness. Democracy emancipated us from the caprice of individual tyrants. But it made the nation more powerful than it was in the days of personal government. Tyrants ceased their wars when their exchequers were emptied, but democratic government can levy taxes upon unborn generations and thus continue warfare long after a stage of practical insolvency has been reached. Rapid means of communication make centralization of authority over vast masses of men possible. Thus science and democracy co-operate in making government at once more stable and more centralized and therefore more potent for good and for evil. If we cannot eliminate international anarchy from world civilization, this simply means that we have made government more potent for evil. Mediæval peasants were left practically uncorrupted by hatred through the feudal struggles of their day. A modern war sows seeds of hatred in the hearts of even the children; and our vaunted science gives us the weapons to transmute this hatred into effective and wholesale murder.

Nationalism is not of itself an evil thing. It is not evil that men should organize their social life. It is natural and inevitable. But if one unit of this social life, the nation, sets itself up as final and absolute because it happens to be larger than the others, though not large enough to include the whole human family, then the nation becomes a peril to human happiness. It is such a peril today. It demands the sacrifice of human and personal values, and makes claims upon lives of eternal significance for ends that have no eternal value. Trade routes and spheres of influence, markets and sources of raw material, instinctive hatreds and instinctive fears, imperial ambitions and economic greed, these are the secular motives and the secular aims for which human life is degraded. Nothing can defeat the arrant secularism of our present international order (or it would be better to say our international anarchy) than an appreciation of human beings as divinely and eternally significant souls.

Nations were made for men and not men for nations. If we could see human beings from the perspective of Jesus we would not hold them in contempt nor in fear, and we would soon bring the nationalism which degrades and corrupts their lives under the dominion of the soul.

These big cities in which we live and of which we are so inordinately proud should be regarded with more suspicion and less veneration by the men whose servants they are expected to be. We are as foolishly proud of the size of our cities as of the strength of our nations. What difference does it make whether the city in which I live has a hundred thousand or a million inhabitants? It means overcrowded schools, unassimilated populations, profiteering in real estate, pitifully small apartments and imperiled family life and all the other evils which attend the overcrowded metropolis. How puerile we are in our vanity over our cities. We recount the story of their rapid growth to every passing stranger.

But we forget that we never built them for men. We build the factories first and the men stream in from the farms and from across the seas to seek work there. Providing these men with homes and comforts and cultural advantages is an afterthought with most of us. We make it as difficult, in fact, as we know how for these newcomers to gain a foothold in our city. If we have a shrewd suspicion that the city will grow in a certain direction we make haste to buy real estate there so that we may sell it to the newcomer at a profit. The ethical implications of this practice seem to escape us entirely.

I am not competent to weigh the virtues of rural with those of urban life, but I am convinced that the impersonal relationships of a city are not conducive to the highest morality. Most of us are what we are because of a certain amount of social pressure and social influence. If the individual is completely detached from his social group and lives an isolated life, as he frequently does in the metropolis, it is not easy to maintain the highest form of virtue. No man can estimate the number of moral tragedies which the loneliness of a big city occasions. We are, of course, not totally blind to this problem of the city, and we try in church and lodge and club to personalize the relationships of the city. But our efforts are hardly diligent and far-reaching enough to accomplish the purpose. There are social thinkers who think that the large city is hopeless and that the only hope for an industrial civilization is to decentralize industry and destroy the metropolis. Perhaps they are right. Whether they are or not, our immediate problem is to do more than we have done to make the city a servant of men. If we have a sincerely spiritual interest in men, we must insist with greater passion and more effective social action that cities were made for men and not men for cities.

Industry is another of these dangerously ambitious servants of man which is constantly setting up its own life as an end in itself. Ideally the modern machine with its multiplied productivity should be a blessing to man. It should provide him with more comforts and more leisure. To a certain extent it has done that.

The eight-hour day is the fruit not of legislation, but of labor-saving machinery. Our comforts have certainly been increased tremendously by machine industry. But no one seems concerned to note the price we have paid for these blessings. Creative joy has been taken out of work by the automatic machine. The cultural advantages which were inherent in many forms of toil in the hand-craft period have been destroyed. The more we have humanized the machine the more have we dehumanized the mechanic and given him nothing in return but a fairly decent wage and the doubtful blessing of an automobile. We have a naïve delight in making and owning things. It is not easy to recognize the personality of the worker in a big factory, but we have not even tried to do it. Every form of industrial democracy is anathema with us because we fear that it will retard production. Everything is sacrificed for efficiency, mechanical efficiency. No industralist gives a second's thought to the inevitable tendency of modern industry to destroy the cultural advantages of toil and leave the laborer without even a desire for a richer and fuller life. If labor does express some dissatisfaction with the terms of its employment, we set that down as rank ingratitude. We are paying good wages, and we do not see what more these ingrates want.

We fail to see that the possession of the things which modern industry produces is not an unmixed blessing. It is nice, to be sure, to have the vacuum cleaners, radios, phonographs and automobiles, which are the characteristic products of industrial enterprise. But we have become the slaves of these things. They are in the saddle and they ride mankind. We are more comfortable than happy. We conduct our business task with feverish diligence in order that we may have all these things in proper abundance; and then we use them to live as hectically in our leisure as in our business. And we prefer luxurious possessions to necessary ones. How many young men are buying automobiles on the part payment plan, who ought to be saving up their money for a house? That is one reason for the housing shortage and the little apartments in which it is quite impossible to raise a family.

Modern industry is a problem not only for the producer and consumer, but for the community as such. For industry aggravates national frictions and is one of the roots of war. The hungry maw of the great machine must be fed, and so we post o'er land and ocean for raw materials and do violence to the backward peoples who possess the materials which we need for our industrial enterprise. Our worry only starts with raw materials, for we need markets as well. The big machine is constantly producing more than we consume, no matter how high we raise our standard of living. Consequently we must find world areas into which these excess products can be thrown. Thus inevitably we find industry behind every kind of imperialism. What a vicious circle we are in. We sacrifice personality for the production of things; we sacrifice serenity and quiet in the use of the things made at so great a price; and then we imperil peace with our brothers as we try to impose our things upon the less-favored portion of mankind. Surely it is time to say with force that industry was made for man and not man for industry.

Of course, it is easier to say that than to recognize industry in terms of its principle. The fact is that our industrialism and our nationalism and our urbanism are all intermeshed so that the real question for modern man to solve is whether he wants civilization to be for man or man for civilization. Our conquest of nature and the resulting wealth, our rapid means of communication and the resulting centralization of authority within nations and increased intimacy of contact between nations, our great industrial units and the resulting inequality of privilege and power, all these characteristics of our modern life have made civilization a very dubious blessing. We are comfortable, but we are not happy; we are living hectic but not abundant lives; we have leisure, but no capacity to enjoy it; we have a world neighborhood, but no world brotherhood. We shall probably secure none of the things we really need until we regard our whole modern life with less naïve delight. We are too uncritical about it. We have permitted civilization to become our master through the same weakness which raised servants to tyrants in other days. To make civilization again the servant of man will require a penetrating insight on the one hand and a robust faith on the other. The people who really believe in human values, and who hold to a transcendent conception of the soul must be more sophisticated in dealing with the enemies of the soul; and the people who know modern civilization and have discerned its general tendencies with acute penetration need more faith in men. The soul has no victorious champion because its friends do not understand its enemies; and those who understand its enemies do not believe in the soul.

Logically, religion should be the final champion of personality. For it is only a world view which is grounded in religious faith that can properly appreciate the precious mite of personality which man must defend against impersonal nature, and again against an impersonal nature that it has not learned the art or acquired the interest to champion the soul against the oppressions of civilization. That is why so many humble folks who suffer most from the weaknesses of modern civilization are disavowing religion. That is why labor is growing cynical throughout the world. Nothing will convert it from that cynicism but a religion which can prove itself socially and morally effective, which can bring our economic and international life under the dominion of the interests of the soul.

We need people with such a consistently spiritual appreciation of human life that they will instinctively oppose every social custom and every political institution which dwarfs and degrades men. If the factory robs men of personal values it must be changed until it builds character and creates happiness. If the city imperils virtue it may have to be destroyed, providing it cannot be reformed. If the nation outrages the diviner qualities of human life and sacrifices eternal values for petty ends, it must be reformed until it becomes a true servant of human personality.

To accomplish these herculean tasks we need a very robust faith. Only a strong faith in men as children of God, rooted in a spiritual conception of the universe, will prompt men to champion the cause of the soul against the world. But this faith must be as discerning as it is robust. The enemies of the soul all profess friendship for it, so that naïvete in the champions of the soul becomes a besetting sin. It is not easy to penetrate through the conscious and unconscious hypocrisies of modern civilization. Only the force of a robust faith and the keenness of a trained intellect will do it. If we can maintain our faith and put in its service the best social intelligence, we will be able, in time, to refashion our civilization into something akin to the Kingdom of God. If we fail in either spiritual passion or moral intelligence, our vaunted civilization will become a huge Moloch which will devour our children. Let us look through the eyes of Jesus with His cool discernment upon all our social customs and traditions, upon all our economic practices and industrial methods, upon our great communities of race and class and ask: Are these man's servants or his oppressors?

PRAYER

Our God and Father of us all, we pray Thee that we may come to know the worth of man, and that we may come to understand that the mission of Jesus was to bring to man a way of life which is above the physical. Teach us the true dignity of man. Help us to find the joy there is in giving to our lives the importance which Thy Son has ascribed to them. Help us to find the joy which follows a definite will and program to bring abundant living to the world where we live. Grant that the Christ may find in us willing workers, ready to take determined stand against every power of tradition and present tendency which would narrow the vision and beat back the progress and the larger life of men. We ask in His name. Amen.

[The text of "Winning the World," delivered in Buffalo, New York at the Sixth National Convention of the Evangelical Brotherhood on August 22, 1926, was printed in the convention report.]

28. "Winning the World"

I have as a text this evening just the prayer of our Lord, "Thy Kingdom Come."

Being gathered in convention as Christian people, it is natural we should ask ourselves the question: "What are we here for, beside wishing to see Niagara Falls?" I do not say this to be facetious, but to show that all motives are mixed. We come together as Christian people in whatever association we activate, to define and re-define our object; another aim is to improve our techniques in reaching our object; still another is to inspire serious pursuit of the object. Now it may be necessary to improve our technique, it may be necessary to inspire. To a certain extent inspiration is inevitable, so I would rather speak on objectives instead of improving techniques or any effort to inspire, in order to see reallly what we want to do.

We are a gathering of men, chiefly. Our immediate objective is Bigger and Better Brotherhoods, and that is a simple American way of doing it. A German and an American were asked to write on Elephants. The German entitled his book "Elephants— Their Habitats, History and Habits," the American simply wrote, "Bigger and Better Elephants." We want bigger and better Brotherhoods immediately. We should often ask, What is the Brotherhood for?—which we do not always do. All organizations are dangerous at times. All organizations that develop through the years experience a period of imperialism, which affects the principle of their being and the fact of their growth. The more we succeed in our Brotherhood, the more we let it go at that. But we should always realize that we want to build our Church through our Brotherhood. We want a Brotherhood that

"WINNING THE WORLD"

serves the congregation, and also the denomination. We are still hectic and frantic, trying to win over the congregation to the denomination, and as soon as we effect this the denomination cannot be anything, because it does not win more people to Christianity. *Our final end is to win men to Christ with the distinct aim to follow Him, to form a Christ-like character.*

If we look into the world today as Protestants, we must be impressed with the fact that you cannot build a Christ-like character in an un-Christ-like world. To a certain extent it may be possible to transcend the world in which you live, but it is not altogether possible. We are always corrupted by the world, of which we are a part. This is one of the things we are learning psychologically, and experience has always taught it. We are not altogether ourselves, for personality has layer after layer which are not original, but are general. I may be what I am not only because God gave me a soul, but by what my father and mother were before me, because I was born in America, born in the twentieth century, and because I live in Detroit. The core of my personality may have become something, but ideas and ideals come with the world. And as the world is sinful, I am not going to be free of sin, no matter how honest my motive is. If I live in a world where Satan is, I will not be free from sin. So we have come to the idea that you cannot build a Christ-like character without having a Christ-like world. Jesus meant that when he insisted on establishing the Kingdom of God.

This Kingdom for which Christ asks us to pray in that ideal prayer has historically meant different things. The words "Kingdom of God" have been filled and emptied so often. It has been defined as purity, peace and piety in the individual soul. Others held that the Kingdom would come by a miracle. When the Roman Church was at its height, it was believed that she formed God's kingdom, and that outside of the Church there was no salvation.

The Reformation had at least this meaning that when a sensitive conscience, a sensitive German conscience, saw this Church it said, "We will have no Kingdom like that, there was too much sin in it. We will go back to the old idea of the Apostolic Church. The Kingdom of God is within the heart, let the world go hang."

Then there is the Ascetic idea. The monk said, "I am going to have a Kingdom of Love in the monastery." There were new types of Christians. They scorned the world, that they might achieve salvation. But they made man pagan and monk at the same time.

The latter part of the 18th and early in the 19th century, a new idea of the Kingdom of God arose. The missionary came in our midst, showing wonderful thought and casting an aspersion on the former Christianity. At this time in England among all its industrialism, do we see the Christian developed in the secret heart. Up to this time only the white man became a Christian, probably because he needed it most. We discovered India, China, and Africa, and sent missionaries to win their world for Christ. This "Missionary Movement" started with Wm. Carey and ended with John R. Mott. It is definitely ended. For through world intercourse partly, and partly through the fruits of the missionary enterprise, having cultivated some of the finer spirit and having made contact with other religions, we discovered that the European world was not as Christian as we thought it to be, that our Christianity was not as Christian as we thought it to be. Whatever Rev. Martin Davis, missionary in India, has said here tonight it has proven that the missionary movement has ended. He has shown as fine an insight as any man I know into the fact that the old missionary idea of the Kingdom of God is dead.[1] The conflict is not between Christian and non-Chris-

---

[1]Martin P. Davis, whose address immediately preceded Niebuhr's, concluded that, "Missionaries are not worried as much about India accepting Christ as we are about Europe and America . . . India has seen through us Christians and found many disturbing elements, it is now looking be-

tian, but between the ideals of the Christian and the ideals of the pagan; between the ideals of the Christian in the occident and the so-called pagan in the orient. Let us not use the name Christian. If we use that word we immediately symbolize the very thing against which orientalism is amalgamated.

In America we do not realize today there is enough for everybody. Certainly we are more greedy than India, as Brother Davis has indicated. We count happiness not in standards of life, but in standards of living. We cannot imagine being without an automobile. I cannot imagine myself happy without my automobile. I know that that is the part of the Western world, and not of the Kingdom of God.

I do not see that any profession is free from greed. But you do have altruistic professions. It is true that the ministry is powerful in its altruism. There are some others. There is a difference as between those who want to live off their fellow men and those who live for their fellow men. Many who call themselves Christians are on the wrong side of the battle. We cannot talk of the geographical gifts of God in a geographical but a cultural way. If you love anybody, do not think that stamps you a Christian. Love is a natural instance, not only in the human heart, but in animals. If you love in a little group you have only enlarged this kind of love. If you move at the machinations of your small frantic group you have missed the ideal of Christ. When the World War broke out, the non-Christian world said, "Is that Christianity, that they destroy the children of the Kingdom of God." To those who believe in psychology, and who also believe in spirituality it is significant that the one man who

---

yond us and beginning to behold the divine Christ Himself in all His Holiness and Majesty. In other words, India is now turning to Christ, not because we claim to be His disciples, but by the virtue of what He Himself is . . ." See Rev. M.P. Davis, "Winning the Men of India," *Report of the Sixth National Convention of the Evangelical Brotherhood, August 22-25, 1926, Buffalo, New York*, p. 91.

believes in the "Sermon on the Mount," who believes that the only way to overcome evil is to smother it, is Mahatma Gandhi. Nothing is as distinctive as the looming of this figure on the horizon of the world, a man who says he is not a Christian, but follows Christ; who proves that the fight is not between those who have accepted Christ and those who have not, but those who do not understand the genius of Christ. People still believe that war is the ultimate arbitration. Here in America, the safest nation on earth, we spent last year 650 million dollars for armaments, and if anybody rises and says that is exorbitant, he is told he is a fool. We have not understood the elemental fact that when you mistrust somebody else; then you increase those elements in his life that are worthy of mistrust.

I do not mean that you can overcome evil by smiling at it; the gospel according to "St. Polly Anna" sickens me. You are not going to overcome evil by walking genially through life. Psychologically a person is only the sublimation of the brute in us. If we now kill by machine guns instead of scratching their eyes out as formally, we are not better. The first fray is between those who believe in service, and those who practice greed; those who practice love and those who practice hatred; those who believe in spiritual forces and those who cling to the material; those who believe in the Lord and those who do not.

Some will say that finally I have become orthodox, we finally agree with him; and others will say, at last we disagree. I do not want to be more orthodox than the epistle of St. James, who wrote that the devils also believe. I know there are people who believe in God, whose deeds are different from their creeds, and so many people are better than their creeds.

[The following two addresses, the texts of which were printed in the convention report, were presented at the Tenth National Convention of the Evangelical League at Milwaukee, Wisconsin which convened from August 7-12, 1928.]

29. An Aristocracy of Spiritual and Moral Life

I am a preacher and so I can't very well speak without a text. The text I want to use is very well known, but I want to use the modern translation: "Ye are the salt of the earth, if the salt becomes insipid what good is it?"

I don't believe that Jesus thought that his disciples would ever be in the majority. It is true that he mentioned the great tree where the birds of the heaven could rest, but he also used other parables, in which his disciples are a creative minority going out into all society. Zwangwill said: "Christianity is a religion for the minority which has been corrupted because it has been forced upon the majority." Jesus said that his followers were to be leaven, to be salt, to be a minority, and minorities at all times worked out to be of the aristocratic type.

Now as good democrats we do not like the word aristocracy, which we believe means a privileged people. The fact is that society has always had aristocracies, that is people who knew how to do things other people could not do. There are aristocrats in every church, in every League, in every unit of society, the proportion of aristocrats being about one-tenth to one-third.

There have been aristocracies of land and privilege, there have been aristocracies of intellect, there have been aristocracies of art, and there have been spiritual aristocracies, and I think that Jesus said to his followers: "You are to be a small group within a large group and are to influence the latter by a unique life, by unique positions and habits of mind that come with being at peace with God and your fellowmen." Ye are the salt of the earth.

It is an interesting thing that every aristocracy has degenerated including even spiritual and moral aristocracies. As a matter of fact aristocracies are in a continuous process of degeneration.

There is not any Christian church nor any League that is not under temptation of sacrificing its principles, or diluting its faith in order to become more popular. The institution or organization becomes a thing in itself. An interesting thing about an aristocracy is that there is the tendency that its achievements become hereditary. When we have accomplished something we like to pass it on to our children, whether they merit it or not. Napoleon looked upon every monarch with contempt, saying he thought no more of them than of any other human beings just because they were of purple blood. Nevertheless he spent half of his time contemplating how, if he had an heir, he could crown that heir.

Now this curious inconsistency in Napoleon's life is something you will find in every Christian life. One of the reasons we are not more Christian than we are is that we have tried to inherit from our fathers what you can not inherit, for the truth is that the finer and more spiritual things are, the less you can bequeath them. None of us are as good Christians as we ought to be, because we are born into Christianity and are never faced with a critical position of deciding for Christ. The missionaries tell us, and rightly so, that some of their Christians surpass us because they have to make a very definite decision, and have to break with the past and with the world. We just slide into Christianity, and for that reason do not find it so easy to maintain the standards of a virile Christianity.

I do not happen to be a Methodist. I happen to be a Lutheran. We don't expect people to come into the Christian life by a crit-

AN ARISTOCRACY OF SPIRITUAL AND MORAL LIFE

ical decision. Confirmation is based on the acceptance of the idea that if we have been nurtured in a Christian home we ought to be Christians. Nevertheless it cannot be denied that we were confirmed because our parents wished us to be. We are confirmed without being confronted with a decision and may have lost a certain uniqueness that they have achieved who came into the Christian life by a critical experience. The aristocracy of religion is not any different from other aristocracies because it is inherited. Goethe's words: "Was du ererbt von deinen Vätern hast, erwirb es um es zu besitzen," is one of the most spiritual truths.

Another interesting thing about aristocracies is that they can be selfish. They conceive themselves created for the purpose of helping society and finally imagine that society has been created to help and serve them.

We know very well that much is written about a landed aristocracy. Our fathers bore burdens too grievous to be borne. They were made to be slaves. In America there is a landed class of people who have through some achievement gained tremendous wealth, and now place burdens upon the common man too grievous to be borne. They imagine themselves to be the lords of the new day who have the right to demand services of the masses.

The spiritual and moral aristocracies of today are selfish too. They try to gain special blessings from God because of their right. Jonathan Edwards once preached to his people that some day they would see the sinners fried in hell, and that they would praise God when they saw that sight. Such extreme examples are not quite as common today as they once were. One of the most unselfish attitudes ever expressed lies in the prayer of Moses: "If you can't save these people blot me out of thy book of life." In a real sense it is true that none of us are altogether selfish, just as none of us are altogether unselfish.

There is another kind of selfishness. It says: "We are the good people. That is why we are prosperous people. It ought to go well with us." Just a few years ago most people got very enthusiastic over a popular book by Bruce Barton in which he says: "If you want to be a very successful man all you have to do is to follow the Sermon on the Mount. Godliness is profitable for all things." There is nothing so great as the art of eating and still having. There never has been a spiritual aristocracy that has not tried to claim wordly advantages through its privileges. Aristocracy tends to degenerate, to maintain itself through power and instead of saving society expects society to save it.

This is true about the present Christian church. We Protestants usually refer to the Middle Ages as being degenerated. We note very carefully how the Apostolic church degenerated into the Roman Catholic Church. Then we say that Protestantism did away with that degeneration. And now we as Protestants represent a degenerated aristocracy which prides itself on a heritage which is already corrupted. The fact is, of course, that we are sinful. Four hundred years old is the Protestant church, and four hundred years is enough time to let the degenerating and corrupting forces work in the church, and I think it can be said that the Protestant church of today refuses just as much to admit the corruption existing in its ranks as did Roman Catholicism, though it is a different kind of corruption.

I mean to say the gospel states that we should love another— not only those who love us, but those who do not belong to our group and class. The cursing thing is that we love the people who look like us, and that is a nice way of paying ourselves a compliment. Jesus never said that love is a Christian virtue. In our churches and in our preaching we are always claiming that love is a Christian thing. Looking at life, we know that that is not true. It is not a distinctive Christian virtue, nor even a human virtue. We can find love in the animal world. If you just love in your own crowd, if you love those who love you, you are no different than the heathen are.

The distinctive difference is not love, but the extent of it. If you can love people who do not belong to the crowd you belong to, to your church, to your race and class, you are a Christian. If you put that down as the unique mark of a Christian, not many of us will measure up to it.

There are only a few of us who have ever learned to forgive people. This is the natural thing. If someone hurts us, we want to hurt them. We have not the imagination or the intelligence to forgive. No matter how religious you are, it seems to require a certain amount of quick intelligence to love people outside of your crowd. We lack the perspective to see what other people are, what other nations have been, and what others have done.

We have not learned how to deal with our Negro problem, not to speak of the Jews.

The motive of today, the dominant motive, is greed instead of service. People are inclined to be very greedy. One of the reasons for this is that we apply the principle of love to a narrow field. People think it sufficient to love their family, yes, they love their own church group, they serve their church, but they do not see why they should change the world. I heard a wonderful sermon once on Good Friday, the minister had the text of how Christ gave himself for us, and asked that his congregation examine themselves as to what they could and would do for Christ, to make some sacrifice for His sake. Then he followed it up by asking: Can't we have some folks offer their services as ushers, or to pass out song books, and can't some more ladies join our Ladies' Aid Society, and some of the young people be more active at the next ice cream social? That is the kind of sacrifice we are always getting even among the best of us. We don't let our love spread out beyond the family, we want to isolate it within the small group, and that is how the new moral aristocracy is created. People who are making an honest effort to follow Jesus often do not join the church; they point with contempt at such weakness of ours and say: You repeat the words "Lord, Lord" and do not the things he asks of you.

I do not want to make any unqualified statement about the Christian church, for I belong to it as you do, I have helped build it as it is with all its faults and shortcomings. All I ask is: How can I be a Christian without being a hypocrite? Or rather: How can I be a Christian without being too much of a hypocrite? For how can you call yourself by the name of Jesus who incarnated love in such form that it has gone down through the ages without equal, and still have our part in society with its hates, its greeds, and its murders?

I once heard Studdert Kennedy preach a sermon about a fund he was raising for poor children of his parish. He said: I would like to raise 300 pounds, I am going to give 5 pounds myself. The reason why I mention the sum I am donating is because I at least want to be as honest as possible about it. I am leaving on my vacation tomorrow, and I am spending five times that much for my children. So the best I feel I can do about it is to be honest. And then followed one of the shortest and most significant prayers I ever heard: Father in heaven, we are all hypocrites, make us as little hypocritical as possible.

So the question that remains is: How can we save ourselves from hypocrisy? How can we put a measure of sincerity and honesty in this life of ours? I want to make a few suggestions. Do you know that there is not an Evangelical league anywhere that could not have an adventurous experience if they would take the words of Christ regarding love seriously? Do you believe in love? How can you and are you going to recognize and interpret love in your business? How are you going to be a

AN ARISTOCRACY OF SPIRITUAL AND MORAL LIFE

Christian in terms of modern society standards of honesty and sincerity? If you take any one of these, you will find you will have a very interesting meeting. You talk about love in the home; about justice, and everybody believes in justice, but justice applied to what situations? The whole thing is we have not been specific enough. Now when you begin to do that one of the interesting things about it is that you see that the great conflict here is not between the terrible evil and the wonderful good at all. It is not between the highest and that which is not so good. It is not because we have been tempted by some horrible sin (although this is not beyond possibility) but because we have done some one simple thing, have followed the ordinary, mediocre advance instead of charging. We have done the ordinary thing instead of the phenomenal. That is why Jesus said the Kingdom of God is like the man who prepared a feast. Who were they that didn't come? The bad people? No, very good people who had legitimate excuses. One had just bought a yoke of oxen. This was not a crime. Here was a legitimate thing of life in conflict with some higher thing of life. Another had just bought a farm. It isn't a crime to farm a farm. But he put a lesser good against an ultimate good. The third had married a wife, and that isn't a crime either, at least I don't think so. But in every case, and there you have the astute intelligence of Jesus, there lay a conflict that barred them from the Kingdom of God, not because of the love of evil, but because there was no real love for God, not because of the love of evil, but because there was not real love for the highest good. If you let the ordinary things of life turn you from the astute intelligence which will take in the principles of Jesus, then how are you going to be a Christian in business? How are you going to be Christian in your homes. There are a great many people who imagine themselves Christians that haven't the smallest idea of the application of Christian principles in the complex existence of today.

John Howard preached very forcefully for the reform of the

prisons in a day when prisoners were treated like animals. Now the love of God was in that man's heart. He was a wonderful man, I doubt if any man ever did more for the Kingdom of God than he did in his way. Yet just before he was married he wrote a letter to his bride somewhat like this: "I think it will be well that we understand beforehand that conflicts will arise between us, so I think we should make an agreement that when such conflicts of will arise, my will shall prevail." All of us may be Christian in a certain situation without agreeing to be Christians in another. Christian principles are not transferred automatically from one situation to another. That is why we need not only preaching but also these discussion groups where we have opportunity to analyze and compare and examine.

But it is not only this new intelligence for which I am pleading, for if we want to save ourselves from the corruption of moral aristocracy we need the spiritual power which we can receive only through Jesus. I know it is not only rational, because many know these things and yet cannot be true Christians because they are too rational, too sophisticated. You have to be something of a fool. If you are altogether common sense you are not fool enough to love as Jesus would have us, you cannot give as he taught us to do. Love must be blind in details, it must be able to catch the general worth and appreciation of personality. There is something at the heart of all Christian virtues, something that comes out of prayer, and that is why the future of the church depends not only on the new intelligence that young people must create, but also on that inner control that comes through the indwelling of the spirit of Jesus.

Finally, the choice we have to make is a choice of will. Some people believe and said that if you would tell young people all about sex, you would have a new day of sex morality. Today they know all about it. There is an immense amount of that

AN ARISTOCRACY OF SPIRITUAL AND MORAL LIFE

information such as our forefathers never thought of. But contrary to expectation we have more morality problems than ever before. We should have knowledge, and more knowledge in that field than in any other field. Nevertheless you will have to admit that the will must be there, and that is simply an emotional, volitional, and religious problem.

Open Forum Period

Question: What would you consider the most effective process of establishing a new Christian morality?

Reply: Not only one way; but rather two things must go together. First increasing spirituality, secondly through the more honest and intelligent application of Christian principles to specific problems. The more complex life becomes the greater need for intelligence. I would say for our young people's work one of the most unfortunate things in our class, in our Leagues, is that we so often mimic the preaching service. The League group and Bible class group ought to be a group of seekers and searchers, kind of a Quaker meeting, that they get together to figure out the problems of life. I don't think preaching has as much educational value as we think it to have, it only reinforces what people already know to be good. If people do not have a chance to get back, they either say: He does not know what he is talking about, or they say sure, that's true, but never apply it. If we are going to make Christianity mean something in the adjustment of modern life, our League groups ought to be more democratic and more specific. Let the Sermon on the Mount be the heart of the church, but let there be all kinds of classes and fellowships around the various questions.

Question: Can a Christian apply the Golden Rule at all and get along?

Reply: By the way, I don't think much of this emphasis upon the Golden Rule. I will tell you why. The Golden Rule is a frame for a picture. If you put the picture in it that Jesus put in it, it means something. I say, "Do unto others as you would have others do unto you," and if I mean by that only that I will treat other people honestly, that doesn't make me a Christian at all. If I realize that life at its highest point produces love, which means that I give what I have to you, then the Golden Rule begins to have meaning. Some businesses call themselves by the name Golden Rule. This means nothing but an ordinary morality. Some work out more than others. Do not get into conflict with society all the time. Nobody who is in earnest about Christianity is always going to meet earnestness all the time, everywhere, in all sorts of situations.

Jesus insists upon that. Jesus put a price upon martyrdom. He said, "Blessed are ye when men shall curse and revile you and shall say all manner of evil against you falsely for my sake." If you try to follow Jesus' social principles, someone is going to call you a "Bolshevik," or a traitor, or something else. The interesting thing about it is that our own society is based upon compromise.

Society persecutes two types of people. 1) The criminal — they are not good enough to live with us. 2) The interesting thing is that society not only persecutes the fellow who falls below but also the one who rises above. That is why on Calvary there were three crosses—two for the thieves, one for the Christ. And that is not an isolated drama but a historical and cosmic drama. That is the way life works.

Question: Is there anything in the teaching of Christ that cannot be carried out today? Should Christians use the police force, and should they compel people to give them what they have taken away?

Reply: If Jesus is taken literally, he says if they take your coat, give them your overcoat. What are you going to do about all these things?

Someone said they were oriental expressions. Let me tell you, there is not a person on earth even the Bible literalists who do that. The interesting thing is that people who insist that we should take the Bible literally mean by that that we should observe literally what they observe literally. How many wash each other's feet at communion time?

Let me tell you how I conceive them. I believe that Jesus lived his life absolutely by the strategy of love, his crucifixion therefore was an inevitable consequence. If you live that same kind of life that is what will also happen to you. Now our problem is: How far can we live the life that Jesus lived and still stay in society? I would prefer that against being so sure that I am a Christian, I am working at it, perhaps more than ever before. I find that ideals and principles which I seemed to think impossible are becoming standards of today. Another interesting thing is that there are always people to whom the ideal is impractical. At first the ideal always will be impractical, but it finally becomes the standard of the world. "Seek ye first the kingdom of God and all these shall be added unto you," they will grow naturally as time passes. However, "everything shall be added unto you" means if you are not squinting at the things that shall be added unto you.

[Delivered at the Tenth National Convention of the Evangelical League, which met from August 7-12, 1928.]

30. Youth and Religion

It is an interesting thing to watch how spiritual treasures, ideas and ideals, creeds and faiths are transmitted from generation to generation. I recently read a very wonderful book: *The Stream of History*, in which is described how through the ages the various forms of life, of spirit, of culture go down from one generation to the next, with only a slight difference between each one, but glancing over the whole you can distinguish the new things that have been created. Especially in the home life we can tell this. I receive from the atmosphere of the home the ideals and faith of my parents. Seemingly unchanged I accepted them and yet some of my ideals will be different. I think I had accepted everything in the same manner and yet there will be different emphases because the center of emphasis will be changed. So there will always be a certain tension between the generations, between young and old in matters of idealism, custom and belief.

Now this conflict between generations has various causes. There is a natural difference in the religion of young people and older people, just because they are young and old, not because of generation. For the young people will become old people and will have another viewpoint.

There is another difference. The temptations of the young people are temptations to commit sins of the sense. Old people are tempted to commit sins of the mind. Old people commit the sins of greed, and covetousness, and hatred, and pride, while young people are more liable to commit the sins of passion. Now this difference between the young people and the old gives them a sense of disquiet. Old people are always saying that young people are destroying and tearing down the results of their work. Young people are saying that the old people need to be revived.

Both are right. Young people to a certain extent are always reforming the world and to another extent endangering it. It is quite right that old people should say "Be careful. This new way of life is dangerous. Don't you realize that these conventions that you are attending are breaking up the things handed down through the ages of experience?" It is right that old people should say that. It is also right that young people should comment on the world that the old people have built.

Though old people may think that young people have not any religion because it does not express itself in the way it did years ago, the fact is that young people are naturally and intensively religious. There are some people today who think college boys and girls have no religion because it expresses itself in a different way than it used to. Right in this city there gathered two years ago a conference of college students who were discussing the Christian faith—a bigger conference than any conference of college students gathered for any other interest or subject in the last generation. And then there was the large student volunteer convention which met last year. No subject will bring college students together in such large numbers as the subject of our Christian faith. Of course there are a great number of people in our colleges who are living what is called pagan lives. Nevertheless, you can find in the colleges as you can find in other groups, those who are saying to the world and to their fathers, "We want to build a better world." Their minds are not aged. Inevitably as you grow older you begin to accept certain things which you thought bad when you were young.

As you grow older you begin to accept certain things that struck you as queer and odd when you were young. Not many to be exceptions from that. When we start out in life proach the world with the kind of idealism in our mind e nurtured in our family we firmly believe the world is Then we gradually begin to discover the evils and shortngs, and our conscience reacts vividly. We want to change ngs, we want to live up to our ideals. And then as we begin grow older we begin to adapt ourselves and to accept what we once opposed. Hardly any young man enters business who does not discover there some practices, absolutely honest perhaps, yet contrary to his Christian idealism. He says: "That must be changed." And there is no young man who is not tempted to gradually accept standards lower than the ones which he once upheld. So you always have in youth a fresh idealism, a conscience reacting against old vices, which is the re-making of the world. On the other hand we find ourselves revolting against some of the good things handed down to us by the cautious experiences of the past generation. So we find the same generation in conflict with its fathers because the world they built was too good, because it checks the desires which are natural in the hearts of all young people whose blood is warm. In the Youth Movement of Germany we find this conflict expressed stronger than anywhere else.

The youth movement of Germany is a conflict between generations expressed more strongly than anywhere else. The youth of Germany never compromises. They express their ideas and ideals in an absolute form. This conflict between youth and age expresses itself there as in no other country. The *Wandervögel* are on the one hand accusing the old people of ruining this world. They say to them, "You brought about the world war. We want a world without war. You created a world in which there are class divisions and race prejudices. We want a world without these evils." These Wandervögel have taken in people of all classes and faiths. It is a conflict between the old and the young in which each is partly right. The world is moving onward all the time. What appeared to be good and perfect yesterday is not good today unless applied in a new way. What works out well now may not work quite so well tomorrow.

If I am exactly like my father was, I am not as good as my father was because his virtue fitted his day and it won't fit my day so well. I met a young German a few weeks ago—one of the finest and most brilliant business men I have ever met. He told me his father controlled a factory in Berlin which employed some 15,000 people. His father had accepted the paternal ideas of the nineteenth century, had pension funds in his factory, had organizations for the welfare of his workers, and imagined himself a Christian business man of the last word. He said then the world moved along, the war came, the industry of Germany had to be readjusted completely, and his father found his plans did not work any more because the business did not function, and a new strategy was necessary in his business. As soon as he grew up enough to know what it was all about, he began to argue with his father. He told him he would have to employ American business methods, stop making 120 things and specialize. The father said he had wrong ideas and he was going to maintain those principles that had always worked so well in his family, that he was too old to make these readjustments. He told the son to go to America and find out how they were doing things there and then come back and see what changes he can make at home.

That is inevitable. What is good for the fathers is not good for the children. There will always remain the necessity that for each new generation the standards and ideals be adjusted. Take alone the ideal of family life, the changes and ideals taking place here, the ideas and ideals we inherited from our parents won't fit into the modern world any more. No matter how fine our idealism will be, some of us will go and get married and still both work, the mother will take her share of the burden as well as the father, and you have the tremendous problem of adjustment, how to give the children Christian nurture and training, how to preserve the good things the fathers had. Nothing that is good for the fathers is absolutely good for the children unless it is adapted to the new situation.

One might say also that nothing that is true for the fathers is absolutely true for the children if they do not make changes according to the different situations. There were certain Christian virtues which are no longer Christian virtues. People believed in the 19th century that the highest god was "liberty." They wanted to be free. Liberty—Freedom—these were great words. In the world in which we live the welfare of each man is dependent upon the welfare of every other man. Do you think that the type of man who has made great wealth, leaves the city, builds himself a home, and puts a high fence around it, illustrates liberty?

I spoke with a certain preacher in Chicago at lunch the other day. He told me this story. "A few weeks ago the great man in my congregation died. He was a very wealthy man. He had amassed his fortune in this way. He made a contract with the state to build roads. He was supposed to cut the trees and then to have the trees in the strip which he cut if he would build the roads. The trouble was that the state did not specify how wide the roads were to be. He built roads two or three miles wide." Now, perhaps he did not mean to be hypocritical—it may not have occurred to him at all.

I am not going to enlarge any more on this conflict between generations but it is there.

Now if there has always been conflict between the generations, there is a special reason for conflict in our own day. There has been a greater amount of knowledge dumped upon the world in the last 100 years than in all the thousands of years preceding. The change of mental environment between fathers and

YOUTH AND RELIGION

children is greater than it ever has been before. I remember having a pretty little high school girl in my confirmation class a few years ago who questioned everything. She was not cynical and skeptical exactly, but just in a questioning mood. She had read her history, and knew more about it than her mother ever knew. Her mother was just worried to death about her. She used to come to me about twice a month and say to me, "What in the world is going to become of my girl. She doesn't seem to be pious at all." And I would say to her, "Don't worry about her. She'll be all right, for she has a natural inclination for religion." The old mother carried on pathetically about this chick, who was more like a duck than a chick, who was living in a different environment than she was living in, but the young girl came out of that period of extreme confusion and I think I can say, though she hasn't reached her maturity yet, there isn't anybody whose future I regard with more promise than that of this young girl. She is a real Christian, and is going to make her contribution to the Christian church. She expresses herself in an entirely different way, and one of the glorious things is that mother and daughter have adjusted themselves to each other, and have made this transition which so often issues in tragedy in a wonderful way.

There is also a great problem for our generation that our fathers did not have because society has changed so much more rapidly, particularly for our own denomination. I remember how 12 years ago when I attended the first League Convention the language problem was one of the great difficulties, a problem that today has lost much of its significance. Furthermore our fathers were immigrants and we were Americans. This caused conflict and called for certain adjustments that other young people did not have to make. Sometimes these transitions did not happen without tragedy, often because the fathers could not adjust themselves. But happily most of those conflicts are past and we are living in harmony, both old and young. Then we must consider that we have an entirely new mental and physical environment. Most of our fathers were farm people and we are mostly city people, the moralities of the city are different than those of the countryside. You realize how the standards and conventions have changed.

A new problem is before us as young people, how are we going to express ourselves, be honest with ourselves, and yet maintain the best of the past? The thought is expressed well in these lines:

"To thine own self be true,
And it will follow as the night the day!
Thou canst not then be false to any man."

Will Durant has written a book called "The Transition," in which he tells how he was raised to be a Catholic priest in a French-Canadian home and how he gradually got into the new world of learning and found it impossible to go into the priesthood. His good father and mother were the souls of piety. He had never had an unkind word from his parents in all his life. Nevertheless, his father told him to leave home. His father spoke the first unkind word when he said, "Get out of this home and never darken its doors again." His heart was bruised to think that religious prejudices could cause his father to say a thing like that. He thought, "I am going to simulate the faith of my fathers. I am going to act as if I believed what they believe." But then he thought that this would be dangerous. It is always dangerous to be dishonest. Years passed and then he speaks of the wonderful conciliation that took place. His parents discovered that his ideas weren't as bad as they thought they were. He was expressing his ideas in a new but no less authentic way.

The conflict is not always as outstanding as this one between Will Durant and his times, but however great it may be, we do have to be true to ourselves. But we don't have to be proud or arrogant about what the fathers have brought. What I don't like about the youth movement is that the youth movement is always revolting, and when you revolt against government you are always throwing out the good with the bad. There are some things that our fathers have built up which are eternal, and if we monkey with them, we are monkeying with the eternal things. Some of the things that our fathers called together, some of the ideals they have worked out in family life, some of the things they stood for in the church are always good. If you destroy them, you are destroying a part of that upon which the Kingdom of God is built, and if in your revolt against the past you say nothing can be good except what is born of your generation, you are bound to be wrong. The rebel is always a destroyer. I was listening to a bright young professor the other day who actually said that all conventions of the past were built upon a superstition, and now that we were wise, we should build a new society upon a new life.

Now of course that is absolute bunk. However, much the new generation may add to the experiences of the past you may be sure that the past has made permanent contributions to our Christian welfare and faith. To a certain extent everything that we can ever learn by our own experience has already been worked out before by past generations. There is no new adventure that we embark on that not someone else has tried before. Someone will tell you about the new morality, you can find that that has been tried out in some other generation. We don't want to be rebels, but we don't want to be slaves either. This is one of the great tragedies of life, that every new generation makes strenuous efforts to improve the world it inherits and then makes the mistake to say: "Now it's perfect." Every generation lives under the illusion that it has created perfection and from now on it must preserve what it has created.

The young people have the wonderful opportunity of making the right transition from the old to the new. In Jesus we find a hold which carries us through both old and new. We who are Christians have a wonderful opportunity to give something to both the old and the new generations because our faith gives us a hold upon a personality that transcends all ages. There is something about Jesus that is not altogether related to the past and that transcends all generations. We may express our loyalty to Him in different ways. So many people worship and follow Him in different ways. I am sorry that I cannot spend the rest of my life in the ministry of congregations. The wonderful thing about congregations is that you don't have just one type. It is a wonderful thing if you have a group of young people who get together to discuss their own problems, a group of men, and a group of women, and a group of factory workers, if you will, and all finally coming together in a common devotion, a common discipleship in Jesus Christ.

["Christianizing International Relations," presented on the eve of his moving to Union Seminary, served as a fitting testament to Niebuhr's maturing thought. It was delivered on September 18, 1928 at the Seventh National Convention of the Evangelical Brotherhood in Indianapolis, Indiana.]

31. Christianizing International Relations

I don't suppose that there is any nation in the world which is really and truly a Christian nation. No group has ever been *wholly* Christian; no individual in a group has been wholly Christian in the matter of the group's racial, national, political problems and relations. We might go further and say that many groups have failed to be just; we can go further and say that many groups have failed to be religious. We violate the ordinary standards of justice.

The fact is that of all the problems of people, *the business of living decently with other people is the most difficult of all.* It is a great task to bring the varied characteristics of individuals within a group into some sort of harmonious contact. All the hopes and fears, the dreams and ambitions, the expectations of the individual within the group, and of the groups as a whole, tend to make this a difficult task. It has been the rule of old for the strong man to command the weak and inevitably to exterminate them. The strong man justified himself for this extermination *in the name of order.* The king and pope of old have insisted that they did certain things not because they wanted to live off the people but because somebody had to keep order.

The Law of the Jungle

There is no Christian world-fellowship. It is an interesting thing, how, claiming to be Christian, few of us are purely Christian in all the intricacies of life. John Howard, a finely educated lawyer, wrote his bride-to-be, "In every home there is conflict. In order to have harmony after we are married, whenever there is a difference of opinion, my opinion shall prevail." It is a fact, homes were once bound together by a more or less autocratic control. To a certain extent we maintain order in them today in that way. Sometimes it is male control. But when the homes trying to bring about a more harmonious and happy relation, find it a difficult task to solve the problems of intimate relations, what can the church expect to do for the other relations of life?

Business is not only autocratic, but there is conflict between the various organizations. These complications are qualified more and more by cooperation. Certainly in the world of business the law of Christ is not used to such a great extent as *the Law of the Jungle*—"Dog eats dog." Inevitably this chaotic way of life leads to an autocracy in which the strong exterminates the weak. Of course the weak may refuse to remain weak, and may unite and make themselves strong. But the society thus built upon violence and force is no better than the autocracy.

Even when we build *international societies* in that way, we find inevitably that violence or force of arms brings mutual distrust; mistrust turns into hate; hatred leads to murder. We need a state of society where people are going to stop this business of exterminating the weak and establish some kind of society from chaos.

The most interesting thing is that this strategic application of *justice is mistaken by a good many people for Christianity.* It is not Christianity. We might call it stoicism. Most people try to be just and imagine themselves Christian. The society tries to be just, tries to divide right from right, tries to keep every man from infringing on other people's rights. The idea is to give each man freedom. One man said his freedom stopped where the man's nose begins. We manage to get along without getting into courts simply by assuming certain standards of justice. All judiciary bodies attempt to define right. You can't define rights very carefully, can't decide a right over a right. Why sometimes *my right actually takes in the other fellow's nose.*

Take our divorce cases from instance. A prominent judge said that the most interesting thing about these divorce cases is that the charges are usually so petty. Rights are so intermingled in these intimate relations of life that it is practically impossible to make a clear decision. When folks get into conflict and cases come into court the judge therefore often bases his decisions on precedent. He is not absolutely sure.

Love Not Justice

Where does Christianity come in? The Gospel definitely pits the idea of *love against the idea of justice.* Jesus refused to divide between the brothers. They come to him with their grievance. One brother said that he did not get as much as his brother from the estate. On the basis of justice he was quite right in coming to Jesus. He said, "Can't you persuade my brother to deal justly with me, and give me my rightful portion of inheritance." But Jesus said, "Who has set Me as a judge over you."

We believe in *the strategy of life where people sacrifice their rights for each other.* It seems to be a very foolish thing to do until you discover when you sacrifice for some one else's right, they sacrifice their right for you, and you gain—a Brotherhood.

Have you ever realized that the most successful families are those with the fewest rules? *Did you ever hear of a family with a constitution*—a constitution signed by husband and wife when married, and the children had to subscribe to it when they were born? That sort of a thing is not done. In an ideal family life, where there is understanding of each other's rights, *love solves the difficulties* and the incipient signs of friction before justice has to take hold. The family relation must ultimately become the basic relation of all men in order to establish the Fatherhood of God and the Brotherhood of Man. You can define the whole of Christianity in those terms. Man has made standards of justice—human standards of conduct—justice against love. This is far from a Christian measure.

The bigger the group gets, the more intricate its problems; the less Christian are its relations. In the first place, *are we decent in our relations within a group?* Hardly any of us learn to be decent to those outside our group. The tragic thing is that we are all right to those in our group; those who think as we think, look the way we look, act as we act. This is a fine way of complimenting ourselves. But how about decency toward other groups—people in other racial, religious, and national groups? Here is the complication. Individuals find it difficult to deal justly with others within the group. How much more difficult is it for the group as such to be decent in its international relations?

The Danger of Loyalty

You can see what happens when I give myself unreservedly to my nation. I am liable to feed the selfishness of the nation in that way and grow a dislike and distrust of other peoples.

Take our children in our schools. We think we have to implant the loyalty idea. We carefully exclude from the schoolbooks anything that would seem to give a critical note to our nation's history, in order that the child might properly love its nation. We encourage the idea—our nation has done nothing wrong, no other nation has done anything right. This uncritical attitude is what has made our nation un-Christian! I remember very well that I was in college before I heard that there was anything to be said on the other side in the War of the Revolution. And I was a senior in high school before I learned that the Southern people had a right to object to Sherman's march to the sea. The idea was that I must think that everything our nation had ever done was 100% right. And so I was raised to be a Jingo as most of you were. Individuals in loyalty to their group find it difficult to be critical.

Ignorance Breeds Contempt

It is very *hard to be decent to people you don't know*, particularly when they are different from what you imagine them to be.

It was so with the Jews and the Gentiles, the Greeks and the barbarians. The term "stranger," "foreigner," has ever had a connotation of contempt. *We, in America, are parochial.* The German people and the English receive a wider education in international relations. Every morning they receive the news through their papers. So far as I know, there are only two papers which give this kind of information in America. Again, I say, we are parochial. We do not know what is going on in the world at large. We have no way of putting ourselves in other people's places. Kindness is a word that comes from, and is related to, the word "kin," according to etomologists. But here is the great difficulty, to be kind to the people with whom we have no physical contact.

Romain Roland tells the story of an oriental scientist. This man had a very delicate instrument by which he could see the pulse beat in plants. He made a public test in Paris. He took a crowd to demonstrate the use of the instrument. He placed a turnip in a vessel of water. He said, "I am going to show you how the pulse of a plant beats. I will put a little poison in. At first this accelerates the pulse, but finally, after the addition of more and more poison it stops the pulse, and kills the plant just as in the case of human beings." The scientist poured a little poison in and the group noted that the pulse was accelerated. Gradually he poured more and more until a boy in the gallery called out, "Don't kill it." The intelligence of this scientist and his explanation had brought the understanding of plant life so close to the mind of the boy in the gallery that he did not want to see it die. This is the way of life. There is not one of us today who would be so indecent as to refuse to our neighbor whom we know and see bread and soup if he were hungry. But not so to those we do not know.

Christian Standards for Nations

We have come *from the way of violence to the way of justice.* America has refused to enter the League of Nations and the World Court. We recognize that the whole world has made progress and points of friction have been eliminated. But yet we do not have peace. We must bring nations under the Christian standard. *The latest attempt is through the "Outlawry of War"* by which nations convenant with each other for universal peace. There are two ways of considering this covenant—two temptations that confront us.

The first temptation is that of being overcome by a sense of futility, *the feeling that it is impossible,* that it cannot be done. When you see how difficult it is to solve the problems of family life, there is a temptation to pessimism regarding the making of nations Christian. How can we bring the nations of the world into the realm of brotherhood when we have not solved the problems of intimate relations?

Then there is a temptation to *an undue optimism.* We thought that to win the nations of the world to peace, "Outlawry of War" was the thing. That was an ideal gesture. We said it about the League of Nations. According to this outlawry of war covenant nations promise to be friends. That does not mean that they are going to be. Of course there is efficacy in a sacrament of friendship. Why do we shake hands? Would not just a smile be all right? This physical sacrament is more effective. A sacrament is an outward sign of an inward thing. There has never been a sacrament of repentance that produced such an absolutely pure inward repentance, yet the ritual is important. No one can dare deny its spiritual efficacy.

This convenant, this sacrament of friendship, is *a sacrament of mutual trust*. They come together and say, "We trust each other now, we are going to outlaw war. We are not going to wage war against each other any more." I claim that was an advance. But it raises the question, how great an advance will it be? It is wonderful for those who hope to have peace. If one nation breaks the oath we can say, "Didn't you covenant?" "Didn't you promise?" It is a wonderful thing for the Christian nations to have this promise as their aid.

Outlawry of War

But let us consider for a moment *the weakness that discounts the optimism of a covenant*. This does not mean that war is abolished. The League of Nations hopes to do this. The Outlawry of War agreement does not make any distinction between wars of defense or of aggression. It is a play upon words. The League of Nations did not meet our need, so we wanted a new agreement, thus this "War Outlawry." But it does not make a positive statement about defensive war. Suppose a nation decides that it is going to war and that it is a war of defense. It is up to the other nations to decide, all the other nations have freedom of action. The situation is quite obvious. Wars of defense on international situations grow out of mutual relations—physical aggression of one and spiritual aggression on part of the other. The World War was called a war of defense.

Perhaps Europe accepted the idea of Outlawry of War because it came from America. Europe accepted it as the advice of a rich but not too intelligent uncle. The nations of Europe thought about it in this way: "America has been on the outside of the whole thing until now. We want her to come in on any terms."

But each nation made reservations. They did not write them into the treaty but made them by correspondence. France said, "We will sign the covenant not to make war on any nation, within the bounds of those treaties previously made." Now according to previous treaties France will have a right to use force under the case of aggression. England said, "We accept the covenant but we want everybody to understand that within the region of the British Empire we may find it necessary to use force and the covenant shall not apply in that instance." The European nations felt that America would very shrewdly and carefully sign the covenant, with the agreement that the outlawry of war would not interfere with the Monroe Doctrine. *They were good mind readers.* We have got troops in Nicaragua.

Nation Must Sacrifice for Nation

How difficult it is to be brotherly! I know a man who has won real laurels in this outlawry of war movement. He was the unofficial ambassador of America to England when the treaty was signed. He is a fine Christian man and I admire him very much. When England made their reservation he said to the British people, "You spoil it all. We wanted to have something pure, something absolutely without blemish. You reserve the right to use force." Our European friends said, "You don't mean to say that America did not have this reservation in mind from the very beginning, that they did not intend to make a reservation with regards to the Monroe Doctrine?" In absolute innocency he raised his hands to heaven and exclaimed, "I am sure no such idea is in Secretary Kellogg's mind!" This made the English, French and Germans hold up their hands in a gesture of despair. They said, "Why don't you Americans talk specifically? You talk in abstracts. How are we ever going to understand each other?" And they were right. For while he was solemnly raising his hands to heaven, *we did have those troops in Nicaragua.* Thus we can see how difficult it is even for good people to attempt the Christianizing of international relations—to be not only just but imaginative and loving. For love is finally nothing more than justice plus imagination.

One is almost overcome by a sense of despair. There can never be a final peace until there will be nations, who can in the moments of crisis, actually *sacrifice their own rights for the good of the world.* But, suggest that today to decent people and they are almost ready to stone you. The Chicago Tribune is ready to send you back where you came from—wherever that is. George Washington said, and this has been the general idea through all the ages, "No nation may be trusted beyond its interests." It has always been *national selfishness against the rights of the world.*

That was *a beautiful expression of Christian sentiment,* we just heard sung by the chorus. It is interesting to know the way in which it was written. Kipling was one of the arch-imperialists of the last century. On the day of Queen Victoria's Diamond Jubilee he beheld the wonderful sight of the review of the British fleet. Instead of being impressed by it, he was struck with awe and humility and repentence. He said to himself, "Is it possible that the British Empire has lost sight of God?" He wrote this poem of confession, just sung:

> "The tumult and the shouting dies,
> The captains and the kings depart,
> Still stands thine ancient sacrifice,
> An humble and a contrite heart.
> For heathen heart that puts her trust
> In reeking tube and iron shard,
> All valiant dust that builds on dust,
> And guarding, calls not thee to guard;
> For frantic boasts and foolish word,
> Thy mercy on thy people, Lord."

But this is the peculiar thing. After he wrote the beautiful thing, he threw it into the waste basket. His wife rescued it and that is why it could be sung tonight. (Many a man has been rescued for Christianity by his good wife.)

This is a perfect illustration of the way the whole world is turning. Once in a while we catch a glimpse of that brotherhood which will make all men children of God. In all the intricate and complex problems of today, with the ruthless application to the practical, *nations must be made to see and to submit themselves to the dominion of the Christ Spirit of service and sacrifice.*

[This condensed stenographic transcript from an address delivered on October 13, 1929 was made at the General Conference of the Evangelical Synod of North America, held in Rochester, New York. As in some of the previous essays in this collection, Niebuhr alluded to the role that tradition plays in inter-generational religious understandings. It was printed in the February, 1930 issue of *Light Bearer*.]

32. The Traditions of the Fathers and the Virtues of the Children

Jesus said: "Every scribe who instructs in the Kingdom of God is like a householder who brings out of his treasure things old and new."

It is the business of each new generation to determine what things new and what things old it is going to bring forth out of the treasure. We live our lives; our fathers' lived theirs. They had certain experiences and trod certain roads, and a path has been worn on them. Some of the roadways are the wrong roads. They have tried them and found out and they have turned back, and if we in our generation know about life, we will find out about these wrong roads that our fathers did tread, and also turn back. We will learn by our fathers. Each new generation has its own insights. It is not an easy matter to determine how much we will accept of the tradition of our fathers and how much we are going to live by our own experiences. To a certain extent the fathers have a distinct belief that if things are old they are good and the young people believe if they are new they are good.

Our fathers have had certain experiences and believe what they say is right and good and true. Our sons and daughters will see that some of these things are true, but they will say they have had such and such an experience and that this is a new day and these old traditions are not good in this new day. There has always been a certain tension between generations. Today that conflict is accentuated because the conditions under which men live and the mental atmosphere they breathe change more rapidly than at any other time.

One writer expressing the conflict between the generations gives us this:

> "Said the old men to the young men,
> 'Who will set you free?'
> Said the young men to the old men,
> 'We.'
> Said the old men to the young men,
> 'It is finished, you may go.'
> Said the young men to the old men,
> 'No.'
> Said the old men to the young men,
> 'What is there left to do?'
> Said the young men to the old men,
> 'You!'"

We are hoping that the conflict is not going to produce that kind of a spirit and attitude, but the tension is bound to remain. And the problem of each new generation is essentially the same: how much of the traditions, customs and faith of the fathers shall it accept and preserve inviolate; how much shall it reject and how much shall it hold and begin anew.

If you look at the life of Jesus you will note that he tried and tread on various ways. He wasn't consistent about the way he dealt with the prophets and the laws. Sometimes he said, "It is said unto you of old . . . but I say unto you." Sometimes he set himself against the laws and the customs of his day. Sometimes he accepted some of them and said they must be absolutely fulfilled. Sometimes he established new laws that he said were going to be better, if any changes were to be made they would be more rigorous.

And sometimes he did an interesting thing, he destroyed the

THE TRADITIONS OF FATHERS AND THE VIRTUES OF CHILDREN

traditions of the fathers in order to accept those of the grandfathers. He emancipated himself of immediate traditions by going to older traditions.

There are young people who simply accept the old traditions without questioning them, but not so many. No matter how good the old ways are you have to work them up and experience them yourself. They remain second hand propositions if not worked out by you. You can't get anywhere by traditions alone, you have to adjust traditions and customs to your own experiences.

But any young person who starts out with the idea that anything that is old is automatically barred and anything that is new is good, is going to make a wreck of his life. I know of a group of young people, university graduates, who as students came to college out of traditional homes. Upon arriving at college they discovered that a great deal they believed was not in accord with modern culture. They said: "What's the use, nothing is really good and nothing really evil unless we make it so." They gave up all their old ideas and made new plans and now that whole group is living in chaotic circumstances. Not one is making his own living, they are all being supported by father or mother. If that is the result it would be best if they would not go to college.

There are too many people going to college today. We need education. We need more all of the time. But there are too many going to college who should not be there. They become interested in destroying the old but are not energetic and intelligent enough to create the new. There are beauties of life that we must maintain against the new tendency. We can't destroy the old with complete disregard. Some tendencies in this day are bad and in our fathers' days were right. But we are so anxious to establish our new traditions that we have been unfair to the traditions that our fathers brought to this land.

There is a Hungarian cabinet maker who lives near my home. He refinishes old furniture and makes new things. He is like an artist, he delights in making things. But he does not make very much money. I discovered this when he did some work for me. I asked him how he could make money with the small charge he made and asked him why he did not go into a furniture factory. He said he could not do that because there was no artistry in that; that in a factory they had to go through a regular routine, but that he liked to create things himself. He said there were four generations of cabinet makers from which he came down. I asked him what his son did. He looked sort of downhearted and said he was selling real estate. Now his son may have been selling real estate and making a great deal of money, but that was the tragedy. That son may make millions of dollars and may be able to build a house of God with some of his money, but I would like to worship in the fellowship of the cabinet maker. After that we took flowers to him from our garden and we discovered he appreciated them and considered them adequate pay. He certainly has the real Christian spirit.

We went to a Polish settlement house at one time. We were asked if we did not want to go upstairs where they said in one of the rooms were a few of the Polish young people maintaining some of their folk dances. We went up and there were about twelve Polish young people who were maintaining their fathers' dances, their fathers' traditions. Downstairs there were three hundred dancing the modern jazz dances. These twelve were not ashamed of their fathers' traditions. There was better stuff in them than in those who had cast the traditions aside.

We can take for example our own lives. A good many of us are of German extraction. We have been so very anxious to obscure our German traditions and to prove that we are Americans. The more completely we are American in some respects the less Christian we are. A psychologist recently wrote a book, the first three

THE TRADITIONS OF FATHERS AND THE VIRTUES OF CHILDREN

chapters of which were on the "Americanization of the Soul." They are not very complimentary chapters.

In dealing with the problem of our traditions, history has proven that iconoclasm and slavery to the past are equally mistaken attitudes. The fathers have wrought what is worth preserving. Anyone who imagines that the morals and conventions which discipline and preserve family life are all outmoded simply because we are "living under new conditions" will learn to his sorrow that our conditions do not change some of the permanent facts of human nature. There are some moral traditions of our fathers that must be maintained. Some young people believe that rules that have regulated sex in the past generation haven't any place in the modern life. How often there is a scene between the mother and the daughter on the daughter's social life. Mother will often say, "That isn't the way we used to do it." Daughter will say, "I know it, but that is the way it is done nowadays." Mother sometimes is a back number, but never as completely as daughter imagines. Her traditions may not quite fit, but her words of warning and apprehension are correct. She may not quite be able to understand the new ideas. There is a certain camaraderie between sexes that is beautiful in many ways. Mother doesn't always understand it that way.

There are certain conventions surrounding family life that have been there a long time and that are worth preserving. Some of the things folks want to try today were tried by the Romans and they were a failure. If you look back in your histories you will find some of the results of periods of loose family ties. They failed also in the great experiments in the Renaissance. If you do not take your histories to see what people tried and failed in you will fail also. What good are histories if we do not make use of them?

When you deal with religion you deal with ineffable things

that you can't quite express. People picture a certain thing is good for them and a newer generation comes along and it doesn't quite fit. Each creed needs to be a little different for each generation. Each new generation after living and experiencing insists that its ideals are correct but history proves that the next generation has a new way of expressing itself. And each new generation donates some new religious experience. With that kind of a problem it behooves us to be reverent. We will be reverent with the religious traditions of our fathers. Someone has insisted that one should try with every child to divorce it completely from the past and to have it start entirely new. That cannot be. We must look into the past, but not altogether. We are fools if we do begin some things anew. Every scribe who instructs you brings out of the treasure both old and new. It is something of an adventure.

We cannot afford to accept the traditions of our fathers without amendment. The things that may have been profitable to them may not be for us, because we are living under a new kind of civilization. Our fathers, our American fathers, conquered and possessed this virgin continent and developed an ethic of individualism. They believed in liberty and destroying the conventions of Europe, the traditions and teachings of the state church and all that sort of thing. They believed that liberty was the absolute thing. This is not a world in which liberty is the absolute thing. Interdependence is the thing.

We are dependent upon what everybody else does for our livelihood. We live in a world where every nation depends on every other nation. If the cotton crop in the south is not one hundred percent, the mills in Manchester are out of work. Last week two thousand men who are truckers in New York City went on strike and seven million people in Greater New York were depending on those truckers who transport fruit and

THE TRADITIONS OF FATHERS AND THE VIRTUES OF CHILDREN

produce from one place to another. All of us were threatened with hunger because of a three day strike, a few days more and we would have had no vegetables. Imagine it, seven million people depending upon two thousand truck drivers. That is the kind of world we live in. What everybody does, effects what everybody else does. We must learn the virtues of mutuality and social responsibility.

It makes me smile to see the ado being made over Ramsay MacDonald these days. If he were running for office in America he would be showered with scorn and contempt. Yet he is the most prominent statesman in Europe, and why? Because he has discovered the kind of Christian idealism needed for the new day. He hasn't tried to get ahead of the crowd. He has practiced Christian brotherhood, he has believed that the poor people must be organized. He stayed with the working man, he didn't desert him when he came into power. That is a new kind of idealism and also an old kind of idealism. He has gone back to the past. Through much agony and a great deal of blood-shed we will have to overcome the individualism of our fathers and establish anew social idealism.

Our fathers built nations. Nationalism in conflict with parochial loyalties was a virtue. In a world which has grown into a neighborhood, the national spirit, if it is not sublimated by higher loyalties, has become a vice.

Our fathers knew little of racial goodwill. Racial bigotry and religious intolerance go hand in hand. But we must learn to appreciate the excellencies of other racial groups. One writer after a visit to China states that there are only two possible ways to deal with the racial question. Either to disavow any kind of decency and brave it through with the sword, or to get on a thoroughgoing basis of brotherhood with the rest of the world. A great deal of attention will have to be given the latter to make it effective.

I went to a racial convention where the students were trying to solve the race problems down south. There were southern students and northern students. The southern students were much more conscientious than the northern students. They go through agony of spirit and prayer. These white students go into the meetings with colored students and talk of common problems as of a common people. At one meeting they took a picture of the white and colored students together and the pictures were put on sale. But the northern, white students did not want to buy the pictures; all of them had a glorious time but they were afraid to show their pictures to their fathers and mothers.

We might bring it down to more personal terms, not only national and racial affairs, but in very human relationships, this family problem of ours. The family of the fathers with all its excellencies was essentially an autocracy. The new family must learn to be democratic both in the relationship of husband and wife, and parents and children. While it is true that we do not have the large families that our fathers and mothers had, it is also true that the modern family lives very often in apartment houses, whereas the fathers lived in large houses and sometimes on ancestral estates. The young people have to work their way through until they discover which is the best way in the modern day.

They have this new proposition. They have the proposition of not having enough money to get married, except where both of them work. There are thousands of young people in that fix. They can ask themselves the questions, just what is the Christian ideal for these new conditions, how can we be Christian under the new circumtances, is it right to get married and both work and get accustomed to two incomes so that they do not wish to give it up. The wife continues to work, therefore there are not children and there is no family life without the children,

THE TRADITIONS OF FATHERS AND THE VIRTUES OF CHILDREN

so a good many families break up. If they sat down and asked themselves what is the right thing, we might not have these conditions. But could they solve their problems, we might all ask ourselves what the right thing is.

I went to a students' meeting where they talked about everyday problems. At this meeting one young woman got up and said, "I think this is a real problem that we young people face. We want to get married and haven't enough money and we can't have children if we both work. I mean to get married and mean to work awhile and then I am going to stop working and have three children.

I know that telling you of what this young woman said is probably going to shock some of the older people here to think that young people should discuss such problems, life problems, at a meeting. That young woman was a Christian of the finest type and was dealing realistically with her problem.

All our young people's meetings would be more interesting if we would sit down and frankly talk of the real problems. Not sentimentality and that kind of thing, but life's real problems. The young people should say what is the Christian thing to do and each will make some suggestion and we will come out with a new Christian conscience.

They should discuss the proper kind of relationship and premarital standards between boys and girls. What is a decent kind of convention between the two sexes? In a group meeting that I attended, the girls got up and accused the boys of making it impossible to have nice relationships of the kind they desired and maintain their self-respect, that they must do as the crowd did if they wanted to be popular and have boy companions. Then the boys got up and protested and said it was just the other way round. One boy said, "What we have been doing is that we have been expecting the worst of each other. We have been following what the world has developed, getting our ideas through the movies and the public dance halls. We follow what the world is doing and assume that everybody is like that and don't believe that other people exist."

Any one who speaks of the young people as going to the dogs doesn't know the young people or the kind of problems they solve. The young people of today have the same kind of stuff their fathers had. But, they do accept some new foolish ideas just because they are new and other people are accepting them. We should not accept them without investigation any more than we should discard any part of the creed of former generations without first looking into it. But young people do sometimes follow the crowd. For example, when Judge Lindsay came along with his fool idea of companionate marriage, it took the young people off their feet.

At most all conferences a year ago they finally got to the Judge's fool idea. But at one conference a young woman got up and said: "Don't let this idea fool any of you girls. I have been studying sociology and I find that the male was brought into the family circle with great difficulty. The mother biologically and socially used to have complete responsibility of the children while the father was a roamer, he went out hunting and looking around. After ages of agony the father was brought into the family circle, and now this proposition is simply going to give him a chance to get free again. You girls are accepting this business as a sort of emancipation. You are just ignorant if you do."

When I see that young people are working that way, I am sure that they are going to come out alright. Not all, but on the whole they are going to work around to some solution.

It seems to me that if we are really going to have our young people in social fellowship of the Christian Church we must disallow all sentimentalities and consecrations of vague ideas and get down to the main purpose: What to consider a complete analysis of the kind of world in which we live. How can I live the *happiest* and most *Christian* life in this world? We will have to, on the one hand, appropriate everything the past has given us or we will be *poor* or we will have to take traditions and go ahead. Look into it as honestly as we know how and we will be doing it in the Spirit of Christ.

Our young people's meetings ought to offer us opportunities for a frank discussion of the application of our Christian ideals to the world in which we live. If your young people's meetings in your church are uninteresting, if you have to drum up interest in them by artificial means, the probability is that you are not dealing frankly with the life problems of young people. The curse of our meetings is their uninteresting sentimentality. A frank and honest discussion of the great issues of the day in relation to our Christian faith will make any meeting interesting.

["Religion and Poetry," published in the July, 1930 issue of the *Theological Magazine of the Evangelical Synod of North America*, clearly articulated Niebuhr's belief that vital religion must contain "direct moral and spiritual experience."]

33. Religion and Poetry

It has become fashionable to insist that there is no conflict between religion and science. The victories of science in the last centuries have been so enormous that religious leaders who tried to hold the interest of generations steeped in the scientific world view had no other recourse but to reiterate their convictions, usually quite honestly held, that science and religion, properly conceived have no quarrel with each other. The more the rearguard of religious orthodoxy embarrassed the modern defenders of the faith by their futile efforts to discredit the scientists, the more vigorously have the moderns insisted upon peace with science.

In one sense at least they have been servants of the truth in this insistence. It is impossible to maintain religious faith in the long run by basing it upon the insecure foundations of doubtful history and discredited cosmologies. Science is merely the application of human intelligence to the problem of discovering, analyzing and collating the observable facts in the cosmic process and in human history. Intelligence is not infallible and mistakes have been made and will be made in the scientific effort. But it is idle to judge the truth and falsity of any thesis emerging from scientific observation by its agreement or disagreement with the special interests of religious ideas and revelations. In that sense at least there can be no conflict between religion and science.

Nevertheless it is a too simple solution of the difficulties which religion faces in a scientific world to insist merely upon the desirability of a peace which obviously does not exist and to deprecate a conflict which the obscurantists may have aggravated but which they did not create. The fact is that religion and science will always be in conflict to a certain extent. At least there will be always a measure of tension between them. The conflict is not between the conclusions at which religion and science arrive but between their varying tempers and methods. Science is analytical. It makes a careful analysis of detailed facts and attempts to explain their relation to each other. Religion has its eye not upon the details of life and the minutiae of reality; it is rather a poetic apperception and appreciation of the ottal meaning of reality. Science is in a sense microscopic and religion is telescopic. Religion has been defined by a contemporary philosopher as a "sense of the whole." The difference between the two may be illustrated by the difference between a psychiatric analysis of an individual and the loving appreciation of that individual. Psychoanalytical criticism of personality undoubtedly discovers truth about character which must forever escape the eyes of love, even though love is alleged to be clairvoyant. There are some things we can never know about personalities except a careful and scientific analysis of their behavior is made. Though such an analysis is sometime very disillusioning it may on the other hand become the basis of a new and higher appreciation of an individual. On the other hand it can never issue in the kind of appreciation of the total meaning and value of a personality which it is the genius of love to gain. There is always a chance that love is based upon illusions which an exacter knowledge will dispel. Yet it would be wrong to regard love as a mere sentimentality to which scientific analysis is always superior. Love may be blind upon occasion but sometimes the blindness of love is merely the indifference to minute defects which a high appreciation of general worth is able to prompt.

While there are all types of love, some having a purely physical basis, it is not too much to say that love is essentially poetic and religious, not to say mystical, and that it is not only analogous to but typical of the religious appreciation of life and the cosmos itself. A religion which discovers the half-hidden purpose of life under its superficial chaos, which relates man to a universe with which he seems to be in conflict and which knows how to find values within the confusion of fortune is no less a tool of truth than the science which discovers so much about the details of reality that the very abundance of its knowledge makes the discovery of unities, harmonies, and values impossible. It may be admitted that religion can make greater mistakes than science. It is easier to chart the traffic of a city street and to take the census of a community than to arrive at any valid interpretation of the life and the meaning of the total community. The generalizations and hypotheses of religion are bold and there are always facts which seem to contradict them. That is what easily leads scientists to hold the convictions of religion in contempt; and that also tempts the protagonists of religion to deny some indubitable facts established by science. There will always be a certain conflict between poets and scientists, between those who describe detailed facts and those who seek to apprehend total meanings. Yet the interests of truth demand that both continue in their pursuit of it.

Another reason for conflict is quite apparent. Intelligence deals with reality. Imagination deals with the potential as well as the real. A perfect love sees in the loved ones not only what it is but what it may become. Religion, in a sense, gives us not a picture of the world as it is but the world as it ought to be. It is always possible that religion and poetry, that all the imaginative arts degenerate into sentimentality by obscuring unlovely reality in their anxiety to reveal potential beauties and values in life. Religion must therefore, for its own sake, be under the critical scrutiny of a realistic and unimaginative intelligence. There is always the possibility that we declare to be true what we would like to be true. On the other hand, every potentiality is in a sense a reality. Ideals which are implicit in reality are real and those who discover them help to make them so. Religion is therefore not only discovery but creation when it functions vitally. Not only the poet but the prophet helps to maintain religious vitality. Religion insists that life has meaning when obviously much of life is chaotic. But it achieves meaning through those who act upon the assumption that life can be lived by the guidance of a sublime purpose and that there are clues to this purpose in the cosmos itself. Religion insists that all men are brothers where it is obvious that men are enemies as much as they are brothers. Yet to regard society from the vantage of the assumption that it is a family helps to create those cooperatives attitudes which make it in truth a family.

The difference between religious truth and scientific truth might be defined as the difference between a description of what is and what ought to be and therefore may be. It is at this point that religion becomes more than poetry and relates itself to a moral adventure. At its best it does not only discover but it creates the kind of world which will satisfy man most. For a wholesome culture there must be tension between the scientific temper which takes into account only the present realities, no matter how discouraging, and the religious temper which dreams of the Kingdom of God and speaks of man as a child of God. If that tension is destroyed society faces the dreadful alternatives of a cynical realism which enervates moral vigor or a sentimental and romantic religiosity which is out of touch with the facts. Modern science has revealed a world in which man is an infinitesimal organism existing upon a second rate planet of a second rate sun. He is neither as central to the life of the universe nor as unique a product of it as he imagined. It was inevitable that the destruction of ancient cosmologies with which religious assurances were closely intertwined should have produced a reaction in the temper of the modern mind which discounts everything but spatial and concrete reality. Yet that does not bring us any nearer the truth. However unimportant man may be, judged by physical standards, he is right in insisting that the values of truth, beauty and goodness which develop in his life are as real as the mountains and the planets. Religion is, in a sense, the devotion of man to these values and the insistence that they are real. It is impossible to deal with the world of values without symbolizing them by symbols drawn from the concrete world. That is why poetry is necessary to religion and why religion is itself poetry.

Personality might be defined as that type of reality where the world of things and the world of values meet. From one perspective man is an animal maintaining a precarious existence in a none too sympathetic world. From another viewpoint man is both the creator and the tool of the harmonies of truth, beauty and goodness which arise out of the concrete world and subdue it. While it is not possible to weigh, gauge and analyze these harmonies as exactly as physical scientists measure physical forces it is also not possible to read them out of the universe. Since they represent qualities of reality which elude specific and exact concepts, they must be apprehended and defined through the poetic and imaginative rather than the purely rational faculties. As long as history produces personalities which are more (or at least feel themselves to be more) than mere collocations of geographic and climatic forces, as long as men feel in themselves the power and the urge to transcend creation and create themselves and to discover in the universe that purpose and order which relates it to the purpose and the will which guides their own life, so long will men be incurably religious and will discover and create in their religious moods what they could neither find nor make by science and intelligence alone. The poet is a more dangerous guide than the scientist. He makes mistakes more easily. But as long as he has a method for discovering reality which the scientist cannot find we may be sure that mankind will not dispense with the poet, whatever may be the perils of his leadership.

Of course, religion is not merely poetry. Poetry is sometimes satisfied with a world of fancy. Religion believes that it reaches ultimate reality on the basis of its moral and poetic insights. "Blessed are the pure in heart" said Jesus, "for they shall see God." What this means is simply that we can realize the moral and personal character of the universe, can discover the nature of God through moral and spiritual rather than through intellectual insight. Upon this assertion and this faith all vital religion rests. Vital religion can be satisfied with neither purely intellectual defenses of the idea of God nor with magical revelations of the nature of God. "The Jews require a sign and the Gentiles seek after wisdom," said the Apostle Paul and dismissed both these methods. He found God in the moral and spiritual experience of Jesus. That is where Christians still find God. Or rather it is through that experience that they find him. Pure philosophy can never get beyond the conception of an immanent God who is too completely identified with nature. Unreflective orthodoxy finds God in revelation but does not relate him to the insights and experience of the individual. A vital and moral religion makes all high living, in which prayer is united with moral striving, the constant source of religious revelation.

This does not mean that the moral experience or poetic insights of any one individual are sufficient to reveal God to him. The experience of any one individual is limited and the imaginative capacity is never fully developed. The individual therefore needs the support of the whole experience of the race. He must appropriate those revelations of ultimate truth which came to the best men of every age who saw God through their moral experience and their poetic intuitions. However, any religion which bases its certainty purely upon experiences of others will lose vitality in the end. Like Job, we need to know God not only "by the hearing of the ear" but by some personal revelation. This personal revelation, on the other hand needs the support of more perfect experience. That is why the Christian turns to the Scriptures and is strengthened and refreshed by the testimony of the prophets and above all by the revelation in and through the life of Jesus. But any generation which loses the capacity to find God through insights cultivated in moral experience and poetic imagination will have no more than a desperate or a devitalized religious faith. Thus Jesus breaks with the Pharisees by demanding a religion which is based not only upon the traditions of the past but upon direct moral and spiritual experience. He finds suggestions of God in the family experience. ("If ye then being evil know how to give good gifts unto your children, how much more, etc."). He intimates that no one can pray to God who is not in loving relationship with his fellowmen.

[The following two essays were excerpted from stenographic reports made at the Fifth National Evangelical Sunday School Convention held in Evansville, Indiana from June 24-28, 1931, and were published in the August and September, 1931 issues of the *Light Bearer*.]

34. Christianity At the Dawn of a New Era

I am going to begin this afternoon with a Bible story. Back in the days when the Assyrians were standing in Jerusalem threatening the people of Jerusalem with their advancing armies, much vaster than Israel's, there was a prophet by the name of Isaiah. He was called in the king's chamber and the suggestion was made that they go down to Jerusalem to fight. He said, "Why do you go forth to Egypt for help when the Egyptians are closer in the flesh and not in spirit? Let your strength be quiet and trust in the Lord." Isaiah was the first great pacifist and he told the king and the people that they should not worry too much about the Assyrians. He said that no nation ever fell by military power alone, and that if they would overcome their weaknesses and trust in spiritual power, that they would be able to overcome the Assyrians. The king let himself become persuaded, perhaps because of the message Isaiah had sent to him, but any way the king did not summon the Egyptians and the Assyrians laid seige to Jerusalem. It looked as if Jerusalem would perish.

The king sent two messengers to Jerusalem and began to mock the people and said, "Why do you defend yourself? Other people have tried and have failed. Why do you call upon God? Your God is no better than other people's God." The king of Israel told them not to talk in their own language but when they got to Jerusualem the people were disgusted with them and told them they were having a difficult enough time and told them that if they had anything to say, to talk in their own language. They said we are talking in the language of the people because we want them to understand, we want to talk. This bothered the king of Judea very much. He felt that the morals of his people would be destroyed, and he told them not to use their physical power but to trust in their spiritual strength, a very difficult faith to hold, a faith which not many people would be content to hold. The people took counsel and the king said, "Let us go to Isaiah and ask him about it. He has gotten us into this fix and let him get us out. Let us say to Isaiah, We are living a sorry day. You have given us faith but not enough faith."

Now I would maintain that the day in which we live could be exactly described in the words of the king. We are living in a day when we have some faith but not enough to bring things forth. We are living in a day in which new things are coming to birth, but there is not enough power to bring them to birth. We see the necessity of new things, but we haven't quite the power of the Gospel to bring them forth. The spiritual thing which inspired our fathers and mothers and the moral discipline which guarded their lives are no more. I am speaking of the peculiar and unique enthusiasm of our fathers and the spiritual history of American people. Almost everything that our fathers and mothers did in adopting Christianity for American life is dead today. The great principle of Christianity in that day must be applied to our day, but there is not enough power to do it.

Look at those things by which our fathers lived and see how dead they are. Our fathers were pioneers. They conquered the prairies and in conquering them they had developed such dignity and ability of character that you find only in the people who conquer the soil. There may be some difference among those who fight the cruelties of nature and those that build the civilization upon the soil. Now our fathers had those virtues. They took the Christian Gospel and applied it to the difficulties which they had faced in conquering the vast western prairies of our land. They had the kind of virtues which you find in the gems of the earth. A kind of tragic dignity was about these pioneers. They were spiritual. We are not living as our fathers did; we are not living in their kind of poverty; we don't have the hardships they had. We are living in a generation of vulgarity. We have to have an altogether new technique of life. It is one thing to be a Christian when you are base; perhaps it is easier to learn to be a Christian in poverty and hardships than when you are living in prosperity.

Our civilization has not yet learned how to preserve the finest spiritual values in a day which offers satisfaction for every physical desire. Our fathers were democrats. In the creed of our nation is written that all men are created equal. Then no man ever regarded himself better than another man. Here upon the American soil the creed in the faith of the poet, Robert Burns, came true. "A man is a man for all that." It was partly spiritual faith of our fathers and economic circumstances. There seemed to be no reason why any class should be held in a particular place. There was always room on the top for the ones that wanted to climb. The office boy could become bank president, and each individual could climb, and it was assumed that every man was the equal of every other man in that place. There was something fine in that creed and when America produced Lincoln, the rail splitter, and he became the president of the United States, the society of Europe stopped laughing and realized that there was something to this democratic creed, that it symbolized purity, power and dignity. But years have gone by. Instead of preserving the democratic creed of our fathers and helping our children in trying to find a place in society, we are building up an aristocracy without the qualities of the ancient people. We have not yet been able to work out a new scheme in terms of our civilization. If we are going to preserve the religion and ideas of the Gospel, we will have to apply it to the fact of our industrial civilization.

Our fathers were individualists and individualism is dead or ought to be dead. There is some individualism left, a remnant of it which has no place in our life. What I mean to say is that they believed that every man by his own individualism could make his own way in the world. If he was honest, and decent he would probably be successful. Now our fathers had a right to believe that, it was a fact. When a vast continent like ours was opened up there was always room on the top and if a man was not successful you had some reason to believe that something was wrong. The thrifty man and the temperate man always succeeded.

You remember that in the Epistle there are two words: "Let each man carry his own burden, and let each man carry it once." Our fathers understood this and particularly emphasized the one truth reading "Everybody carry his own burden." When poor are poor, it is due to their lack of virtue. There are thousands of people who are betting their lives away on the stock market. I know a certain man who for the second time since 1921 has lost his home and now has lost his equity on it. He was a thrifty, decent man, who by no fault of his own, is walking the streets trying to protect his family from poverty.

If we cannot develop a technique and a passion for serving others, having an interest in their welfare, then none of us can be happy. If we will not learn that, we cannot have a decent nation. All of our talents and ideas that we have learned must be applied to the civilization which has made us dependent upon one another.

Our fathers were denominationalists. They had good reasons for believing that. Our fathers were Lutherans, Episcopalians, Quakers, or Catholics, and other denominations. All of these

CHRISTIANITY AT THE DAWN OF A NEW ERA

denominations represented economic, social, and political parties which were different. Most of the people were so attached to their particular kind of religion that they honestly believed that you couldn't be saved unless you believed in their particular denomination. We maintain our own denomination but are making slow progress. We know very well that the old days are dead, but we have not enough power to bring forth the new day. After the war, there were many who were going to iron out the difference between denominations but they didn't have the power to do it. They wanted to have but one powerful common denomination, so religion would express itself in ethical terms. But, certainly, there must always be some more generous rule in recognition of brotherhood. We know that to be true, but we have not yet had the power to bring forth its birth.

I am not saying that we should have one religion but I am convinced that many of them are purely axiomatic. Our fathers were Puritans. Their Christian ideas expressed themselves upon the habits of Puritanism. Puritanism extended far beyond the Calvinistic churches. I had a friend tell me among other questions raised about religion that he thought his father was as good a Puritan as there ever was for his father didn't know what the name of a Puritan meant. His father, a large austere man had certain ideals of personal conduct and discipline and all that it implies. They disciplined their children very strictly in religion. They were very severe about discipline in sexual impulses and family relationship. They were rather severe about the observance of the Sabbath, card playing, and dancing, etc. Whatever the weakness the Puritanism may have been, you must admit it added a good deal of charm to our fathers and mothers. John Ruskin, who was born in a Puritan home and who loved it very much, tells us how his mother made him commit every verse of the Bible to memory. She turned all the pictures on the walls to the wall every Sunday for fear that somebody might enjoy beauty on the Sabbath. He didn't accept the faith of his mother, but he was bound to admit that there was a certain charm in it, and that he took it with him on to his grave.

Now compare our day. We have discarded every one of the old customs. We have fewer disciplines. We believe in expressing ourselves. But I will have to admit that there is a certain charm of theory in the modern generation. The theory of self-expression in the modern generation is not quite as terrible as I have painted it. It must be admitted that we have not yet had enough power to bring forth a new tradition by which life can be furthered.

Our fathers had different opinions of right and wrong. Some of the things that our fathers regarded as right and wrong are not wrong but they didn't know what was right and what was wrong. The young people of the modern generation believe it is better to live by freedom than by restraint. They believe that, because they have looked back in history and found some of the traditions that their parents lived by and they called them crazy, but it is better to live by a crazy parent than to have no parent at all. For it is a fact that life must tell; it has to run into some kind of mold and the Puritan faith was better than no faith at all. There has to be enough power to bring forth a new creed of personal conduct.

Our fathers were nationalists. Nationalism was a virtue to you. When it was in conflict in Germany it represented a high form of idealism. It was a virtue for them to be Italian patriots. It was a virtue for them to be Japanese patriots.

Now in all these various peculiar ideas of our fathers, there are some permanent values. We know very well what the needs of our civilization are. We see how the peculiar ideas, not quite revelant to the world in which we live and yet we go on repeating the ancient traditions and giving our loyalty to traditional institutions and ideas. We do not live thoroughly in our day and we do not give ourselves patience in attending to our peculiar problems. We do not yet have the power to go forth. What is lacking in it? I suppose the new civilization in Russia has its points of danger. It is idealistic but ruthless. I would like to build a new civilization, but I must admit that I don't know of any young people in the world who have so much patience as these people have. Some of the inhabitants of Russia are dominated by its new power, and also political power. The young people of Russia are purely idealistic but they haven't any ideal in their own personal life. They haven't any idea of self-expression because there are certain things they want to do and think their life is poured out to the commitment of this idea.

One thing we have to learn is the power of commitment. We study in our schools, we entertain various ideas, and we find that they are in conflict with one another and we ask what is good and what is bad. We ought not to go on a road until we have looked very carefully to see which way to turn. So there must finally be some commitment. In the young generation of our aspiring churches there is not the sense of commitment. We study and study; we look at the Gospel and say it is appealing, there is a charm in it, but we do not commit ourselves. Our commitment is at a dangerous stage. The farther you go upon it the farther all other roads are from you. We might commit ourselves if we were not afraid of it, if we knew it would lead us to God, but young people don't commit themselves and are inclined therefore to shut off the day of Christian life and all that stands for. I don't know if it wouldn't be a good thing to have a little more patience to commit our life. There is no power except the ideas of power. The more ideas, the less power you have. That is why simple people have to change the world, while the sophisticated people stand and watch.

You remember what Jesus said to a young man, "Follow me"

and the young man said, "Allow me first to bury my father." Jesus said "Why do you have to get rid of your father." The man said, "You see I have family responsibility and until my father dies I have no business to do anything else." "I know," said Jesus, "there is always some reason for doing less than the best, once you stop to think." It is necessary to think, but there comes a time when you have got to stop thinking. Life is very complex and you have to slip by it. There are so many roads to take that if you stop to think, you won't go on any one of them. Our generation has to learn the power of commitment, and the power of sacrifice. Don't believe that when you choose the highest in life that it is the highest compliment that can be paid you. What is best in life is in commitment, and if you stop to think, it is used for the highest good for which you committed yourself. Do you remember the excuses the men had for Jesus when he asked them to come to the supper? "I have bought a yoke of oxen, therefore I cannot come." He was excused on account of business affairs to buy oxen. Another said, "I have married a wife, therefore, I cannot come." To marry a wife, that is permissible. Family relations, preoccupations are things which keep us from the highest loyalty. I know that you can't be good in this kind of world without thinking honestly about life. We need among young people a greater and more absolute commitment than we have. We need, if we are to have power to bring it forth, a more tremendous sense of need than we have.

[Delivered at the Fifth National Evangelical Sunday School Convention, held from June 24-28, 1931.]

35. Christian Education and Society

Education is like an anticipation. True education prepares child and adult to meet situations with a minimum of failure and error. Education helps us to anticipate the situations with which we must contend. Education helps us to develop the technique and skill by which we contend in this world. Education helps us to appropriate the experience of our fathers. It would be a sorry thing if each generation had to start altogether anew. The difference between us and the animal world lies at that particular point. We must appropriate the experience of others so that we will not make their errors over again. We must devote our skills, we must anticipate the situations which we meet. We must analyze the world in which we live.

Now, Christian education has to deal particularly with the development of Christian life in our world. It begins, therefore, with certain assumptions and it is the business of Christian education first of all to ground us in that faith and in those suppositions. There are some moderns who believe that you can live without any presuppositions. They say, let us look at all of the facts and then arrive at our conclusions; but the fact is that it is impossible to find certain things in life except you first believe them to be there. It is for this reason that great traditions and great historic faiths are so important. Everything that Jesus stands for can be experienced but we would not dare the experience if he had not stood for it before we did. We must first of all, in our Christian education, anticipate the meaning of the Christian Gospel. We think we know him and yet we do not. There are vast multitudes who are committed to God without living his life, not because they are bad people but for various reasons they have never understood the spirit of Christ. "Ye know not what manner of spirit ye are of" and I suppose he could say that about each one of us. We don't know the distinctive character of the Christian Gospel; we haven't analyzed it; we really haven't appropriated the meaning of it. I don't know whether there is a motive to commit people to Christ in our Sunday schools and churches, to commit people to Christ emotionally and inspiritionally without letting them know the secret as to what the Christian life means. We all know that it means a life of love. More specifically love covers a multitude of sins and love covers also a great deal of enthusiasm that doesn't mean very much. What was this gospel about Jesus? What did he think about life, and about man, and the way men ought to live with one another? There is a gospel of love in that he believed in mutuality of human relations. They should live for each other. Very few of us do that except perhaps in the family relationships. The best we can do usually if you look at our world is not to live for other people, but to be restrained from living at their expense. That is what we mean by justice. When you establish methods of justice by law it is telling people you have certain rights and other people have certain rights. Don't infringe upon their rights and protect yourself so that they won't infringe upon your rights.

What Jesus asks of us is much more than that. He said that we should not only refrain from living at the expense of other people, but that we should live for them, sacrifice our rights for their rights. It might be a good thing if we began by emphasizing that Christianity is impossible and by adding that mankind reaches its highest statues by approximating the impossible. A certain German theologian wrote a book on Jesus, showing that it was quite impossible to realize any of the ideals that Jesus stated in the Sermon on the Mount. He did that in order to prove that the Sermon on the Mount was not for average everyday living. The Catholic Church says that the Sermon on the Mount represents the gospel of perfection. Now as you look at the way we live we have to admit that that is true or seems to be true, but it is also a fact that every one of the things that Jesus stands for is validated by life and if we will just experiment in that direction of life we will find that it isn't altogether impossible. It also means taking your family attitude and trying to send it beyond the family. See the way you deal with people in your family relationships, your attitude toward them, your trust in them, and then see whether you can develop enough spiritual insight so that you can deal with other people as you do with other members of your family We know in the family it is possible to give ourselves to each other. We know it is possible for the strong to help the weak, because that is what a parent does in the long infancy of the child, growing stronger and stronger as education increases. The strong give themselves to the weak and they make the weak strong by doing that. Now out in the world that would be possible too: the strong economic and privileged classes instead of accusing the weak of being weak because of their own limitations, might recognize that they are weak because of society, and hope that the weak might become strong. What we do in the family relationship is not impossible outside, but it is difficult. We are to sacrifice ourselves for each other. Of course somebody could say how do I know that I won't be taken advantage of if I do that? If I sacrifice myself for others is it possible that they won't catch the spirit of love and take advantage of my sacrifice? I thought Jesus meant that if we sacrificed ourselves for others that others would sacrifice themselves for us. The day of love is not so dangerous after all. But I don't think Jesus meant that. We are cautious; we don't take risks; we don't have to. We ought to give ourselves to others without asking whether they would give themselves to us; that might very well mean the cross. So far none of us have really suffered the cross in any real sense. Jesus meant we ought to sacrifice ourselves for others not necessarily because honesty is always the best policy, but that is the way to live most happily.

The gospel of Jesus is the gospel of love. He believed in trusting people beyond their capacity to justify that trust. If people wrong us we should forgive them, we should look beyond their wrongs and at the possibilities and potentialities of their life. Society punishes him with the mistaken notion that punishment will show him the error of his ways. You ought to do it in another way. If he doesn't change at once you ought to forgive him again, again, and again. You ought to trust him foolishly so that trust would finally become the creative and redemptive force in his life. When we look at the universe and say we believe in God, what do we mean? One of the things we mean is that the universe is not altogether what it seems to be but what it is becoming. It is not the realm of God. Nature is cruel; it makes us blind and makes us ruthless. There are a great many things that do not look like God at all, and you see that the universe is developing in the direction of the idea which is God. The universe is not so much what it is, but what it is becoming. Really and spiritually deal with human beings not according to what you see in them at the present moment but according to the possibilities in them, and of course there are always tremendous possibilities in them that have not been realized. I suppose there are in the group of young people here potentialities of art, science, and religion that could change the world if they could all be exploited. I suppose it could be said that we have not realized our possibilities and that we might possibly realize them more if somebody came along to believe in us, because our decent qualities come out to those who trust us. Our natural instinct is to be careful and afraid, and to protect ourselves against people, for fear they are going to harm us.

CHRISTIAN EDUCATION AND SOCIETY

The Christian religion being a religion of brotherhood, the Christian relation being a mutuality, must drive in the direction of equality, if we are really going to have a Christian society in which all people can enjoy the advantages which are few. Jesus was very vigorous with the people who had many advantages. He said to the rich young man, sell all thou hast and give it to the poor. In our kind of world we are all trying to get special advantages over other people. We do it instinctively. There is hardly one who follows his natural impulses, who does not try to get something that all people can have. The chief charm is that not all people can join that organization. If everybody could get in we'd get out. It is quite obvious that to be vigorous with a brotherly ideal is to share all things with all people. Perhaps that will never be completely realized. Any person who is not trying to bring those privileges to those who do not possess them, can hardly be called a Christian, or be regarded as living in the spirit of Christ. In all these things that you can see, love as mutuality, love as equality, or whether we define love as forgiveness or trust, in all these things we have practically an impossible idea and yet an ideal which can be ground into life and every life can be joyful in the attempt to realize the impossible.

Ought we not in our Sunday classes be dealing with the facts of human nature with a much better and clearer knowledge of what they are and of how brutal the forces of their life may be? The one charge that I make against the church of the modern day is that it is so romantic about human nature. There is a great possibility that we go to church and feel when we come out much better than we really are. But the traditional attitude of the church was to convict people of sin. We don't feel miserable enough in church. We ought to come out of that class every once in a while like Isaiah who said "woe is me, because I am a man of unclean lips and dwell among people of unclean lips." Look at the facts. Here we are at the present time living in a world of economic strife in which there are some six million people unemployed, and I suppose next winter there will be more than eight million. We practice a little charity in order to help these people all over this country, but not enough really to eliminate suffering. In the city in which I live since the unemployment period has begun, there are people finding it almost impossible to live any longer under the terrific depression.

Now I do a little something about that but I don't do enough. If I had more Christian imagination than I possess I would do more. I have an idea that it would be a good thing if the government would ask me and tell me what I ought to do. In other words I wish that in such matters we would establish more social control because we cannot trust self-control. I do not expect this nation, however Christian or non-Christian it may be, to deal adequately with the unemployed in the coming winter except we have much more taxation than we have. We are not imaginative enough to help other people as much as they need help. There is not a single unemployed, if you knew their need, if you saw the sick mother in bed, the children starving, you wouldn't help. But when they tell you there are ten thousand people on the lower east side, fifty thousand people suffering from starvation, I don't do anything about that, you don't do anything about that; we haven't enough imagination to see; we are cruel and ruthless and the world is ruthless. Why, take for instance the relationship between races. Now may I again be pessimistic if you will allow me. I will be pessimistic even if you don't allow me, and say I don't trust myself or anybody else really to be decent to people who belong to a race which is quite different from my own. I can be quite decent to the people who look the way I look, but as soon as somebody looks different I think there is something the matter with them. The reason I act like that is because I am a human being and the limitations of human beings are very difficult to overcome. I know my standards, all the standards of virtue are my standards, and the standards of my group so that when I find people who do not conform to those standards I say they are no good. He may have virtues which I do possess, and may not be as intelligent but he doesn't have any virtues. I say he is no good. I don't hesitate to say whatever the limitations of the negro race may be, and I know that it has limitations, the limitations may be the worst sin which it has ever committed is the obvious difference from our skin which makes it impossible for them to deal with human beings across that line of race. Human beings when they act in groups are indecent to one another.

In the international relation they are so far away we just can't see them. International relations are consistently cruel. Let me give you an illustration right out of the press today. President Hoover demanded a moratorium for the German people saving them from paying some four hundred million dollars a year which they are obligated to pay year after year for fifty-seven years. That is a large sum of money, that means slavery for the German people, and a great nation knows that is true. Economists have pointed out ten years ago that if you would continue to take half a million from the Germans each year you would bleed them white and that is what we have done, but nobody is bothered very much about it. They have almost had to starve to death before we will help and all we said was we will help you for one year and then when you get fed up for a year we will bleed you again. That is really what the policy means at the present time. Life is as cruel as that, just as cruel as that. We can make our Christian enterprises deal more realistically and less brutally. In Germany today you find all the young people, particularly the young people when they express themselves in Christian terms, speaking particularly about the cruelty of mankind and the sin of mankind. We need all the grace which God can give us, all the pedagogical education if we would conquer ourselves. I should think that we ought in our Sunday school classes be making a careful analysis of human emotion and instincts. If you leave us alone we are not going to live for other people, we are going to make other people live for us, and I don't exclude anybody from that. I know some very pious people who could take their servants for granted and make slaves of them to such a degree—they weren't malicious at all, they were just thoughtless. The forces of nature had sway in their life. I don't trust myself upon that matter at all. I think I could let myself go, and sometimes even if I did not let myself go, I live myself at the expense of others. Now the Caesar in you tries to gain greatness by bossing other people, by getting advantage of other people, and by holding other people in contempt so that we can hold our own pride. And we reveal it sometimes even in the most loving relationship.

You realize that even in a loving relationship one person may live at the expense of the other. The stronger will lean upon the weaker. The stronger will make the weak a tool to his decisions and ambitions. There are parents we all know very well who love their children but make all the decisions of their children for them. They live under the illusion that they do this because they are wiser than their children and they like to decide things for other people. I myself have felt the sensation of power when people come to me. I immediately take on the air of omniscience. I feel myself powerful. Life is like that, except under constant discipline. I find we will not live for others but we will make others live for us. Is one person going to make a tool of the other person or is he going to make a friend of the other person? We are all of us naturally vindictive. We don't forget easily. When people wrong us we hold it against them. We say we have forgiven but we haven't forgotten. That really means that we haven't forgiven. Haven't you ever noticed how you gain your self-respect by denying respect of somebody else. It is very difficult for any of us to really assert himself without holding somebody in contempt. Girls who regard themselves as handsome or beautiful if they should find somebody more handsome than they are, are likely to look around for someone that is not so handsome in order to retain their respect. Professors who find those who know more than they do look around real quickly to find somebody who knows less than they do in order that they may preserve their self-respect. Pride is in the human heart and the spirit of love conquers it with great difficulty. We ought to know ourselves. We ought to be taught in our Sunday school classes a clear and more realistic knowledge of human nature and life. We ought to know not only ourselves but the world. We ought to know the forces with which we contend out in the world. Now of course, the world is us, but the reason that we can make a difference between the world and us is this: if you take us one by one we may not be Christian but we are not so terrible, but if you take us ten by ten or one hundred by one hundred we are terrible. The flesh of the devil against which Christianity fights is of course, we ourselves. We may belong to the Christian Church. We may have a measure of it, but the Christian spirit is contending against us particularly when you take us in large groups. However lovely people may be as individuals, if you put them in large groups they breed pestilence everywhere. There again it seems to me that in every individual case we ought to be more pessimistic. As soon as you take a certain economic group, let us say, contending against another economic group, or a certain national group against another national group the denominating forces in that group have been all through history not the spirit of Christ but the spirit of nature, the claw of the tiger and the tooth of the lion. The one thing that we must recognize is that no matter how virtuous we may be we are all servants. If you take us together in our business relationships and our race relationships we are pretty terrible. We ought to be saying to these young people all the time, are we not unprofitable servants. Now that spirit of humility, that realistic interpretation of man, and of history and of facts of society is what seems to me to be more necessary in our Christian education than nickels. Also I am positive if we get to know all of the facts like that it is almost impossible for us to act.

INDEX

A.B. Degree, absence of at Elmhurst, 28, 57-8, 80.
Abele, Ralph C., 25, 38.
Abschiedsredner, 30.
academic standard, importance of, 80, 82-3.
Alhambra, Illinois, 24, 28.
America, relationship of to Europe, 141-4.
"America and Europe," 141-4.
American Seminars, 37, 124, 151.
Americanization, 22, 40, 62-3, 92-4.
Anniversary Record Commemorating the Twenty-Fifth Anniversary of Bethel Evangelical Church, 33.
"An Aristocracy of Spiritual and Moral Life," 179-89.
Arndt, Elmer J.F., 39.
"The Attitude of The Church Towards Present Moral Evils," 30,41-5.

Bacon, Benjamin, 57.
Baldwin, Prime Minister, 126
Baltzer, John, 35, 36, 37, 38, 101, 160.
Barmen Missionshaus, 24.
Barton, Bruce, 182
Basel Mission House, 19.
Bauer, Karl, 119, 120.
Baur, Wilhelm L., 30.
Becker, William, 30, 31.
"*Bedenken in Beziehung auf das Proseminar,*" 120.
Berlin, 128, 154-6.
"Berlin Notes: Impressions of an American in the German Capital," 154-6.
Bethel Evangelical Church, 33, 38.
Bible School, 49, 51.
Bigotry, 215-16.
Bingham, June, 17, 25, 26.
Braun, Theodore C., 38.
Breese, Illinois, 25.
Bretall, R.W., 17, 18.
Brotherhood, 174, 201-2.
Brown, Dean, 54.

Brueggemann, Walter, 30.
Calhoun, John C., 17.
Calvin, 23, 40, 107.
Calvinism, 30, 36, 102, 104, 105-7.
Cambria, Wisconsin, 29.
Carey, Wm., 176.
Carnegie Foundation, 118.
Catechical Instruction. See Christian Education.
Catholic Church, 48, 71-73, 237.
Chicago University Divinity School. See University of Chicago Divinity School.
Children, raising of, 51-2.
Christ Church Cathedral (St. Louis), 124.
Christian Century, 35, 38.
Christian Education, 34, 46-52, 67, 74-78, 84-87, 112-15, 235-244.
"Christian Education and Society," 235-244.
Christian Home, The, 51.
"Christianity at the Dawn of a New Era," 227-234.
"Christianizing International Relations," 199-208.
Church of England, 48.
Church union, 36, 64-68, 101-111.
Cities, 168-69.
Classical education verses modern education, 121-22.
Commission on Closer Relations with Other Church Bodies, 111.
Commitment, 233-34.
Communion. See Lord's Supper.
Communists in Germany, 129, 133.
Concordia Seminary, 30.
Conference on Organic Union of the Church, 36, 101.
Confirmation, 67, 107-8, 110-11.
Congregational Church, The, 117.
Conversion, 50-2, 110-11.
Corporal punishment, 114.
Courage to Change, 17, 25, 26.

245

Culture, as the goal in education, 113.
Davis, Martin P., 176-7.
Dawes Report, 151-2.
"The Dawn in Europe," 151-3.
Deissman, 57.
Degrees, importance of 28, 57-8, 80.
Denominationalism, 64-6.
"The Despair of Europe," 132-6.
Detroit, Michigan, 33, 34, 175.
deutsche evangelische Emigrantenverein zur Grundung von evangelischen Gemeinden an der Pacifickkuste. See German Evangelical Immigrant Society for the founding of Evangelical Congregations on the Pacific Coast.
Die Deutsche Evangelische Kirchenverein des Westens. See German Evangelical Church Society of the West.
Die Deutsche Evangelische Synode von Nord-Amerika. See German Evangelical Synod of North America.
Dibelius, Otto, 37.
Dinkmeyer, Henry, 28.
Disciples of Christ, 103.
Dixon, California, 24.
Dobschuetz, 57.
Dortmund, 124, 125.
Duesseldorf, 127.
Duisburg, 124.
Dunn, David, 20.
Durant, Will, 196.

Eddy, Sherwood, 37, 124.
Eden College. See Eden Theological Seminary.
Eden Theological Seminary, 22, 29, 37, 41, 57, 58, 116, 145.
Education, higher deficiencies at Elmhurst, 28, 58, 116-18, 119-23. lack of general education among Synod students, 82-3.
"Educational Principles in Church Schools," 112-15.
Edwards, Jonathan, 17, 181.
Eighty Adventurous Years: An Autobiography, 124.
Elmhurst College, 27-28, 29, 36, 116-18, 119-23.
Emmaus Homes, 26.

Emotionalism in religion, 46-52.
Episcopal Church, 103.
Essen, 125.
Ethos & Ecumenism, An Evangelical Blend: A History of Eden Theological Seminary, 1925-1975, 30.
Evangelical and Reformed Church, 36, 112.
Evangelical Church in Germany, 21, 59, 60, 64.
The Evangelical Church, 21.
The Evangelical Herald, 124, 128, 132, 137, 141, 151, 154, 157.
Evangelical Synod. See German Evangelical Synod of North America.
The Evangelical Teacher, 34, 74, 84.
Der Evangelische Diakonissen-Herold, 26.
Die Evangelische Synode von Nord-Amerika und die Logenfrage, 26.
Evangelischer Katechismus, 67.
Evil, 41-45.

Fauth, Robert T., 29.
Federal Council of Churches, 35.
Fifth National Convention of the Evangelical Brotherhood, 160.
Financial problems in denominational education, 81-2, 117.
First World War, 34-5, 88-100.
Ford, Henry, 27.
Fourteen Points, 142.
France, 124-7, 130, 133-4, 142-4, 151-3.
Frederick William III, 21.
Freedom in modern teaching, 114.
Friedens Church (Wright City, Missouri), 26.
Der Friedensbote, 22, 31.
"The Future of Our Seminaries," 79-83.

Gandhi, Mahatma, 178.
Garrison, William Lloyd, 98.
General Assembly of the Presbyterian Church in the U.S.A., 36, 101.
General War Time Commission, 35, 89.
The German Church on the American Frontier, 20.
German Evangelical Church Society of the West, 20-21, 22, 24.

German Evangelical Immigrant Society for the Founding of Evangelical Congregations on the Pacific Coast, 24.
German Evangelical Synod of North America, 19-23, 24, 26, 29, 31, 33, 34, 35, 39, 40, 67, 101-11. History of, 19-23. Debt owed to Niebuhr, 39. Niebuhr's understanding of, 59-63, 67.
German Lutheran Churches, 48.
German theological influence at Yale, 57.
Germany, 37-8, 124-7, 128-31, 132-6, 137-40, 141-4, 152-3, 154-6, 158-9, 163, 192.
"Germany in Despair," 128-31.
Geschichte der Deutschen Evangelischen Synode von Nord-Amerika, 20.
Geschichte des Religiosen Lebens in der Deutschen Evangelischen Synode von Nord-Amerika, 20.
Goebel, George, 31.
Goethe, 23, 24, 181.
Golden Rule, 187-8.
Government, 166-7.
Graeper, F. H., 21.
Gravois settlement (near St. Louis, Missouri), 20.
Gunkel, 57.

Harnack, Adolf von, 29.
Henninger, W.F., 109-111.
The Heritage of the Reformation, 39.
Herriot, 152, 157.
High school diploma, importance of, 80, 82.
History, importance of, 83, 202, 213.
A History of the Evangelical and Reformed Church, 20.
History of the Theological Seminary of the Evangelical Church, 30.
Holtzman, 57.
Holy Ghost Church (St. Louis), 38.
Hoover, Herbert, 241.
Hosto, Edward J., 24.
Howard, John, 185-6, 199-200.
Human nature, 182-189, 241-4.
Hypocrisy, 184-6.

Immigration, 19.

"In Rebuttal, by the Author of 'Where Shall We Go?'", 109-11.
Industry, 169-72; effect upon workers, 169-70.
Innerlichkeit, 23.
"Intellectual Autobiography," 17, 18, 32.
"Is Europe on the Way to Peace?", 157-9.
Isolationism, 141.

Jahrbuch des Evang. Proseminars, 27.
Jordan, David Starr, 54.
The Journal of Presbyterian History, 34.
Jungk, Wm. Theo., 31.
Justice, 185, 200-202.

Kamphausen, H., 20.
Kegley, C.W., 17, 18.
Kellogg, 206.
Kennedy, Studdert, 184.
The Keryx, 30, 31, 36, 41, 46, 53, 79, 95, 116, 118, 145.
"The Keryx and Our Educational Institutions," 36, 116-18.
Kettlehut, Theo., 31.
Keynes, 142.
Kipling, 66, 207-8.
Kirchenverein. See German Evangelical Church Society of the West.
Knox, John, 107.
Koeln, 127, 137.
Krupp, 125.
Kruse, Cornelius, 28, 54.

Landon, H.R., 17.
Language question in the German Evangelical Synod of North America, 22, 92-4, 120, 195.
Law of the Jungle, 199-200.
League of Nations, 143, 204-5.
Leaves from the Notebook of a Tamed Cynic, 13, 14, 15, 34, 37.
Leland Stanford University. See Stanford University.
Lincoln, Abraham, 27, 98, 229.
Lincoln High School, 27.
Lincoln, Illinois, 26.
Lincoln Lyceum, 30, 46.
Lindenwood College, 25.

Lindsay, Judge, 218.
Lloyd George, 132.
Lodge Question, 26.
Logenfrage. See Lodge Question.
London, 126, 127, 151, 157.
London Conference, 157-9.
London News, 151.
Lord's Supper, 106.
Love, 162-3, 176, 182-6, 188, 189, 201-2, 221-2, 236-8.
Loyalty, to America, 89-91. Danger of, 202-3.
Luther, 13, 40, 69-70, 98, 106, 107.
Lutheran Church, Missouri Synod, 30, 117.
Lutheranism, 19, 21, 65, 101-2, 104-7.

MacDonald, Ramsay, 151-2, 215.
Macintosh, D.C., 33.
Maeystown, Illinois, 24.
Magazin fur Evangelische Theologie und Kirche, 101, 109, 111.
Marchen von den sieben Schwaben, 31.
Marthasville, Missouri, 22, 26.
Marx, 157.
Mayer, F., 120, 123.
Mehlville, Missouri, 20.
Mennonites, 58.
Merkley, Paul, 17.
"A Message from Reinhold Niebuhr," 35, 95-100.
Messenger of Peace, 24.
Methodism, 65, 110, 146, 180.
Minutes of the Elmhurst Class of 1910/Eden Class of 1913, 31.
Missionary movement, 176-7.
Missouri Synod. See Lutheran Church, Missouri Synod.
"A Modern Sunday School," 84-7.
Monroe Doctrine, 206.
Moralism, 23.
Morality, 41-45; relation of religion to, 41-5. Spirituality as a source of, 67. In Germany, 155-6. Moral (religious) experience, 225-6.
Morgenthau, Hans, 17.
Mott, John R., 176.
Murray, Sir Gilbert, 126.

Napoleon, 180.
Nationalism, 167-8, 202-3, 215, 232-3.
Negro denominations, 118.
New Haven, Connecticut, 31.
New York City, 39, 214.
Nicaragua, 206, 207.
Niebuhr, Gustav, 24, 25, 26, 31, 33.
Niebuhr, Helmut Richard, 24, 28, 31, 39, 53.
Niebuhr, Hulda, 24.
Niebuhr, Lydia Hosto, 24-25.
Niebuhr, Reinhold, his thought as Evangelical, 23, 67-8. At Elmhurst, 27-8. At Eden, 29-31. Ordination, 31. At Yale, 32-33, 53-8. And Bethel Church, 33-4, work in Christian Education, 34, 74-8, 84-7, 112-15, 190-98, 235-44. And First World War, 34-5, 88-94, 95-100. And church union, 36, 101-8, 109-11. And synodical educational institutions, 36-7, 79-83, 116-18, 119-23, 160-64. European travels, 37-8, 124-44, 151-59. Offered *Christian Century* assoc. editorship, 38. Impact of Evangelical Synod on Niebuhr's theology, 40, and social problems, 41-5, 165-73, 174-8, 179-80. And international relations, 199-208, and tradition, 59-63, 190-98, 98 209-19, 227-34.
Nollau, Louis, 20.

"On Academic Vagabondage," 36, 145-50.
Organic union. See church union.
"Our Educational Program," 160-64.
Outlawry of War, 205-7.

Pacifism, 37-8, and patriotism, 95-100.
Page, Kirby, 37, 124.
Painleve, 134.
Patriotism in the First World War, 88-100.
Patterson, Bob E., 17.
Personality, development of in education, 113. Religion as the champion of, 172.
Pflug, Harold A., 38.
Pharisees, 45.
Philadelphia, 36, 101.

Poetry, its relationship to religion, 220-26.
Poincare, 134, 151, 152.
Postville Court House (in Lincoln, Illinois), 27.
Preachers and Preaching in Detroit, 165.
Presbyterian Church in the U.S.A., 36, 101.
"The Present Day Task of the Sunday School," 35, 88-94.
Press, Samuel D., 23, 24, 25, 28, 32, 40, 65. Brief biographical sketch, 29-30. Niebuhr's tribute to, 29. Progress in Christian Education, 84-7.
Proseminar. See Elmhurst College.
Protestantism, 182.
Provincialism in education, 145-50.
Prussia, 21, 59-60.
Puritanism, 166, 231-2.

Quakers, 99, 117, 230.
Record of Ordinations for the German Evangelical Synod of North America, 31.
Reflections on the End of an Era, 23.
Reformation, 19, 21, 59, 69-73, 176.
Reformationsfest, 33.
"A Reformationsfest Sermon," 69-73.
Reformed Church in the United States, 13, 111.
Reinhold Niebuhr. See Niebuhr, Reinhold.
Reinhold Niebuhr: A Political Account, 17.
Reinhold Niebuhr: A Prophetic Voice in Our Times, 17.
Reinhold Niebuhr: His Religious, Social and Political Thought, 17.
Reinhold Niebuhr: Prophet to Politicians, 17.
"Reinhold Niebuhr and the First World War," 34.
Religion, 42, 46-52, 162-3, 172, 220-26.
"Religion and Poetry," 39.
"Religion: Revival and Education," 46-52.
Religious Education. See Christian Education.

Religious experience, 225-6.
The Reminiscences of Reinhold Niebuhr, 17, 18, 25, 32.
Reparation Commission, 152.
Reparations, 151.
Report of the Sixth National Convention of the Evangelical Brotherhood, 177.
Revival, 46-52.
Die Rheinische Republik, 126, 129.
Roland, Romain, 203.
Ruhr, 38, 124-126, 128, 131, 153.
Russell, Bertrand, 98, 159.

Sabbath, 165-6.
St. Charles, Missouri, 25, 26.
St. John Church, 1860-1960, 31.
St. John's Evangelical Church (Lincoln, Illinois), 26, 31.
St. John's Evangelical Church (St. Charles, Missouri), 26.
St. Louis, Missouri, 19, 22.
Scarlett, Will, 37, 124.
Schleiermacher, 21.
Schlussfeier, Eden Class of 1913's, 31.
Schneider, Carl, 20, 21, 30.
Schory, Albert, 20.
Science, education in, 82-3, 119-23, and religion, 220-26.
"The Scylla and Charybdis of Teaching," 74-8.
Second National Convention of Evangelical Sunday Schools, 25, 112.
Second World War, 14-15, 35.
Seeberg, Reinhold, 29.
Sermon, 47, 49, 50.
Sermon on the Mount, 178, 236-7.
Service, 178.
Seventh National Convention of the Evangelical Brotherhood, 199.
"Shall a Minister Have an Education?", 28, 36, 119-23.
Social Evil. See evil.
Spengler, 161.
Spirituality, 44, 67.
Stanford University, 54.
Stone, Ronald H., 17.
The Stream of History, 190.
Stresemann, 134, 135.

Sunday School, 84-7, 112-15.
Teaching, in Sunday School, 74-8, 112-15.
Tenth National Convention of the Evangelical League, 179.
Theological Magazine of the Evangelical Synod of North America, 39, 112, 220.
Tradition, 64-5, 193-8, 209-19, 227-34.
"The Traditions of the Fathers and the Virtues of the Children," 209-19.
The Transition, 196.
"A Trip through the Ruhr," 124-7.
Truth, religious verses, scientific, 223-4.
"Tyrant Servants," 38, 165-73.
Twente, Theophil H., 27.
Union. See church union.
Union Theological Seminary, 18, 39, 199.
United Brethren, 117.
United Church Herald, 25.
United Church of Chirst, 36.
United Lutheran Church in America, 101, 105.
Unity. See church union.
University of Chicago Divinity School, 53.
Untergang des Abendlandes, 161.
Urbanism, 168-9.
Versailles, Treaty of, 157, 158.
Volkspartei, 135.
The Wanderer, 30.
Wandervoegel, 140, 192.
War, 34-5, 88-100, 205.
War Welfare Commission, 34-35, 88-9, 95.
Webster Groves, Missouri, 22.
Weimar Republic, 154.
Weinel, 57.
Weiss, 57.
Weizsaecker, 57.
Wesel, 124.
"What the War Did to My Mind," 35.
"Where Shall We Go?", 36, 101-8.
Whitmore, California, 24.
Wilson, Woodrow, 100, 132.

"Winning the World," 174-8.
"A Woman Named Lydia...", 25.
World War One. See First World War.
Wright City, Missouri, 26.
Y.M.C.A., 53.
Yale Divinity School, 53-8.
"Yale—Eden," 28, 53-8, 79.
Yale School of Religion. See Yale Divinity School.
"Youth and Religion," 190-98.
"The Youth Movement of Germany," 137-40.
Die Zukunft des Proseminars, 119.
Zwangwill, 179.
Zwilling, Paul R., 33.
Zwingli, 59, 106.

4703/079

"These early writings of Reinhold Niebuhr are an important source for understanding the religious and intellectual background of his later commitments and developed thought."
　　　　　　　　　　　　　From the Foreword by John C. Bennett

"Scholarship and research will be enhanced by these articles, particularly in understanding the early, developing Niebuhr—when he was student and then pastor."
　　　　　　　　　　　D. B. Robertson
　　　　　　　　　　　Professor of Religion
　　　　　　　　　　　Syracuse University

"This book is an unexpected and delightful addition to the writings of Reinhold Niebuhr . . ."
　　　　　　　　　　　　　Union Seminary Quarterly Review

"The scholarly community owes a debt of gratitude to William G. Chrystal for his painstaking work in gathering these writings from the Eden Theological Seminary archives and for his helpful introduction."
　　　　　　　　　　　　　Journal of Presbyterian History

William G. Chrystal is pastor of The First Congregational Church (UCC) of Stockton, California. He is the author of *A Father's Mantle: The Legacy of Gustav Niebuhr* (The Pilgrim Press).

The Pilgrim Press　　　　　　　　　　　　　　　　　　　$8.95
New York　　　　　　　　　　　　　　　　ISBN 0-8298-0607-5

Acme
Bookbinding Co., Inc.
100 Cambridge St.
Charlestown, MA 02129

DEC 1 1982